A Nation Prepared:

Teachers for the 21st Century

The Report of the
Task Force on Teaching as a Profession

May, 1986

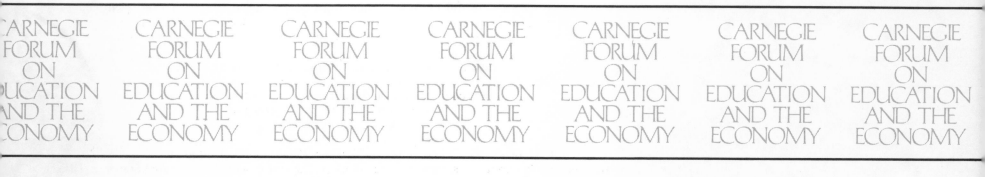

CARNEGIE FORUM ON EDUCATION AND THE ECONOMY   CARNEGIE FORUM ON EDUCATION AND THE ECONOMY   CARNEGIE FORUM ON EDUCATION AND THE ECONOMY   CARNEGIE FORUM ON EDUCATION AND THE ECONOMY   CARNEGIE FORUM ON EDUCATION AND THE ECONOMY   CARNEGIE FORUM ON EDUCATION AND THE ECONOMY   CARNEGIE FORUM ON EDUCATION AND THE ECONOMY

Library of Congress Cataloging in Publication Data

Carnegie Forum on Education and the Economy.
Task Force on Teaching as a Profession.
A nation prepared.

1. Teachers—United States. 2. Teachers, Training of—United States.
3. Teachers' socio-economic status—United States. 4. Education and state—United States. I. Title.
LB1775.C34 1986   371.1'00973   86-11743
ISBN 0-9616685-0-4

The Carnegie Forum on Education and the Economy

The Carnegie Forum on Education and the Economy, a program of Carnegie Corporation of New York, was established in January 1985. The Forum was created to draw America's attention to the link between economic growth and the skills and abilities of the people who contribute to that growth, and to help develop education policies to meet the economic challenges ahead.

David A. Hamburg, President of Carnegie Corporation, chairs the Advisory Council which guides the Forum's activities and provides the core membership of its task forces. The names of the members of the Advisory Council are listed in Appendix A at the end of this report.

The Task Force of Teaching as a Profession

On the recommendation of its Advisory Council, the Forum establishes task forces to examine specific policy issues and to report findings and recommendations to the American people. At its first meeting in March 1985, the Advisory Council recommended that the Forum assemble a group of leading Americans to examine teaching as a profession.

David A. Hamburg, the Forum's Chairman, appointed a 14-member Task Force including several members of the Forum's Advisory Council. Lewis M. Branscomb, Vice President and Chief Scientist of the IBM Corporation, and a member of the Advisory Council, agreed to chair the Task Force, the members of which are listed below.

The Task Force Report

The Task Force's report does not necessarily represent the views of the Trustees or Officers of Carnegie Corporation, or of the Carnegie Forum's Advisory Council. A list of publications prepared for the Task Force, together with ordering information, can be found at the end of this report.

Members of the Task Force on Teaching as a Profession

Lewis M. Branscomb, Chairman
Chief Scientist and Vice-President
International Business Machines Corporation
Armonk, New York

Alan K. Campbell
Vice-Chairman of the Board
  and Executive Vice-President
ARA Services
Philadelphia, Pennsylvania

Mary Hatwood Futrell
President
National Education Association
Washington, D.C.

John W. Gardner
Writer and Consultant
Washington, D.C.

Fred M. Hechinger
President
The New York Times Company Foundation
New York, New York

Bill Honig
Superintendent of Public Instruction
State of California
Sacramento, California

James B. Hunt
Attorney
Poyner & Spruill
Raleigh, North Carolina

Vera Katz
Speaker of the Oregon House
  of Representatives
Salem, Oregon

Thomas H. Kean
Governor of New Jersey
Trenton, New Jersey

Judith E. Lanier
Dean, College of Education
Michigan State University
East Lansing, Michigan

Arthuro Madrid
President
The Tomas Rivera Center
Claremont, California

Shirley M. Malcom
Program Head
Office of Opportunities in Science
American Association for the
  Advancement of Science
Washington, D.C.

Ruth E. Randall
Commissioner of Education
State of Minnesota
Saint Paul, Minnesota

Albert Shanker
President
American Federation of Teachers
Washington, D.C.

Staff of the Carnegie Forum on Education and the Economy

Marc S. Tucker
Executive Director

David R. Mandel
Associate Director

Betsy S. Brown
Staff Associate

Catherine J. Combs
Administrative Assistant

Signatories

Lewis M. Branscomb

Alan K. Campbell

Fred M. Hechinger

Mary Hatwood Futrell

Bill Honig

John W. Gardner

James B. Hunt

Arturo Madrid

Arturo Madrid

Vera Katz

Vera Katz

Shirley M. Malcom

Shirley M. Malcom

Thomas H. Kean

Thomas H. Kean

Ruth E. Randall

Ruth E. Randall

Judith E. Lanier

Judith E. Lanier

Albert Shanker

Albert Shanker

Table of Contents

Executive Summary

Executive Summary

America's ability to compete in world markets is eroding. The productivity growth of our competitors outdistances our own. The capacity of our economy to provide a high standard of living for all our people is increasingly in doubt. As jobs requiring little skill are automated or go offshore, and demand increases for the highly skilled, the pool of educated and skilled people grows smaller and the backwater of the unemployable rises. Large numbers of American children are in limbo — ignorant of the past and unprepared for the future. Many are dropping out — not just out of school but out of productive society.

As in past economic and social crises, Americans turn to education. They rightly demand an improved supply of young people with the knowledge, the spirit, the stamina and the skills to make the nation once again fully competitive — in industry, in commerce, in social justice and progress, and, not least, in the ideas that safeguard a free society.

In the past three years, the American people have made a good beginning in the search for an educational renaissance. They have pointed to educational weaknesses to be corrected; they have outlined ways to recapture a commitment to quality. They have reaffirmed the belief that the aim for greater productivity is not in conflict with the development of independent and creative minds. There is a new consensus on the urgency of making our schools once again the engines of progress, productivity and prosperity.

In this new pursuit of excellence, however, Americans have not yet fully recognized two essential truths: first, that success depends on achieving far more demanding educational standards than we have ever attempted to reach before, and second, that the key to success lies in creating a profession equal to the task — a profession of well-educated teachers prepared to assume new powers and responsibilities to redesign schools for the future. Without a profession possessed of high skills, capabilities, and aspirations, any reforms will be short lived. To build such a profession — to restore the nation's cutting edge — the Task Force calls for sweeping changes in education policy to:

- Create a National Board for Professional Teaching Standards, organized with a regional and state membership structure, to establish high standards for what teachers need to know and be able to do, and to certify teachers who meet that standard.

- Restructure schools to provide a professional environment for teaching, freeing them to decide how best to meet state and local goals for children while holding them accountable for student progress.

- Restructure the teaching force, and introduce a new category of Lead Teachers with the proven ability to provide active leadership in the redesign of the schools and in helping their colleagues to uphold high standards of learning and teaching.

- Require a bachelors degree in the arts and sciences as a prerequisite for the professional study of teaching.

- Develop a new professional curriculum in graduate schools of education leading to a Master in Teaching degree, based on systematic knowledge of teaching and including internships and residencies in the schools.

- Mobilize the nation's resources to prepare minority youngsters for teaching careers.

- Relate incentives for teachers to school-wide student performance, and provide schools with the technology, services and staff essential to teacher productivity.

- Make teachers' salaries and career opportunities competitive with those in other professions.

If our standard of living is to be maintained, if the growth of a permanent underclass is to be averted, if democracy is to function effectively into the next century, our schools must graduate the vast majority of their students with achievement levels long thought possible for only the privileged few. The American mass education system, designed in the early part of the century for a mass-production economy, will not succeed unless it not only raises but redefines the essential standards of excellence and strives to make quality and equality of opportunity compatible with each other.

Preface

Preface *by Lewis M. Branscomb, Chairman*

In January, 1985, the Trustees of Carnegie Corporation of New York established the Carnegie Forum on Education and the Economy. I count it a great privilege to serve on the Forum's Advisory Council which is helping the Corporation's staff define a 10-year agenda to explore the link between economic growth and the education of the people who will make that growth possible.

Among the first acts of the Forum's Advisory Council was a recommendation that the Forum immediately establish a Task Force on Teaching as a Profession. The Task Force, composed of members of the Advisory Council and others distinguished by their standing in education, business, journalism, public service, and science, was created in May, 1985. It was established, according to David A. Hamburg, President of the Corporation, "in recognition of the central role teachers play in the quality of education," and directed to report its findings and recommendations in the spring of 1986 at the first annual meeting of the Forum. This report is the first of a series of policy recommendations on American education to be produced in fulfillment of the Forum's objectives.

Task Force members were not chosen for their agreement on education issues, nor because they stood above the debate. To the contrary. At the risk of making consensus very difficult, we persuaded influential national leaders representing many interests and a range of constituencies to join in the project. Included were governors, leaders of both major teachers' unions, chief state school officers, a leading teacher educator, a state legislator, people deeply committed to quality education for minorities and the poor, business executives and educational statesmen.

We believed that if this group of individuals could agree on the changes necessary in our schools to provide the best chance for higher quality education for all our children, the very fact of this consensus would contribute greatly to the likelihood that the major structural changes required for enduring school improvement would actually come about. No doubt each Task Force member, if writing alone, would have expressed many of our ideas in different words, but this report expresses our common view as clearly as one document by many authors can do.

Four purposes motivated the Task Force in producing this volume: (1) to remind Americans, yet again, of the economic challenges pressing us on all sides; (2) to assert the primacy of education as the foundation of economic growth, equal opportunity and a shared national vision; (3) to reaffirm that the teaching profession is the best hope for establishing new standards of excellence as the hallmark of American education; and (4) to point out that a remarkable window of opportunity lies before us in the next decade to reform education, an opportunity that may not present itself again until well into the next century.

This reform will be expensive. But we are convinced it is affordable. Indeed, if the investment is made over a 10-year period, we need only ensure that our public schools receive no less a share of the Gross National Product than they now enjoy. Even if the nation fails to make this investment, the cost of education will still rise, but the national resources to pay for it will suffer as America becomes increasingly non-competitive in world markets.

In 1910, educator Abraham Flexner transformed medical practice in the United States by insisting on rigorous professional preparation of physicians. Flexner's work, supported by the Carnegie Foundation for the Advancement of Teaching, laid the groundwork for the development of a medical delivery system second to none in the world. That historic Carnegie contribution has paid incalculable benefits to America and its people. We are confident that improvements in the preparation of teachers and the conditions under which they labor will prove as significant to the country and its children.

A Time of Ferment

"As we debate public policies to stimulate economic growth and regain our economic strength, we ought to remember that our public schools are a stronger economic weapon than any monetary theory, trade policy or book on Japanese management. Education generally — the public school in particular — is the most basic source of long-term American productivity and economic well-being."

Governor Bruce Babbitt
Arizona

" . . . if we expect to compete in important areas with those who pay their people [a fraction] of what we pay to assure a decent living standard in our state and our nation, it is absolutely imperative that we do what we can to develop the only major resource we have left, the minds of the people of the U.S. and of Arkansas."

Governor Bill Clinton
Arkansas

"As a nation, and as a state, we are engaged in a protracted economic war of attrition that will not be won with bombers but with blackboards — a war that will not be won or lost on the battlefield but in the classroom."

Governor Richard D. Lamm
Colorado

"Winning the global competition for jobs requires us to retool our schools just as we are retooling our industry."

Governor Robert D. Orr
Indiana

"In the past, prosperity was built largely on strong backs and willing hands. This age puts a premium on intellect and knowledge. It does so through the technology that shapes it and the intellectual skills that drive it."

Governor Martha Layne Collins
Kentucky

"Education is the fuel that drives the engine of economic growth and job creation in America's modern society. In the first 100 years of Minnesota's mining industry, Minnesota supplied half of the iron ore used to build America. I'm determined that Minnesota will again make a tremendous contribution. This time we'll build the economy with our ideas, innovations, technology and our brainpower."

Governor Rudy Perpich
Minnesota

"In Missouri, our primary goal is to create an environment of opportunity, development, and growth for all of our citizens. The two most crucial components in creating this environment are to provide the very best educational opportunities possible for both children and adults, and an aggressive economic development campaign by the state to attract new jobs to Missouri."

Governor John Ashcroft
Missouri

"If the state is going to become serious about industrial recruitment, legislatures and citizens must become serious about improving the quality of our educational system."

Governor Toney Anaya
New Mexico

"I believe that in a global economy, Ohio's ability to overtake our competition is directly linked to the level of our investment in education."

Governor Richard F. Celeste
Ohio

"Better schools is perhaps the major domestic issue today. It's at the center of whether we can become competitive in the world market. That shoots it to the top of the states' list of priorities."

Governor Lamar Alexander
Tennessee

A Time of Ferment

The 1980s will be remembered for two developments: the beginning of a sweeping reassessment of the basis of the nation's economic strength and an outpouring of concern for the quality of American education. The connection between these two streams of thought is strong and growing. They frame the major themes of this report.

The nationwide effort to improve our schools and student achievement rivals those of any period in American history. In a characteristically American way, the initiative was seized by state political leaders, volunteer business groups, local officials, higher education leaders, professional educators, citizens and parents. All sought the causes for a widely perceived decline in the quality of American education while making, each in their own domain, determined efforts to redress the balance.

Much has been accomplished. Course requirements have been stiffened, teachers' salaries raised, and new standards put in place in most states. Partnerships have been formed between the schools and other major institutions in our society which, if they stand the test of time, should strengthen the capacity of the schools and improve the chances of their graduates. Teacher educators have taken the initiative in reexamining the quality of teacher education and are taking steps to improve it. These and many other changes have not come without controversy, and have often been accomplished only by virtue of courageous, determined leadership.

But more will be required, much more than could have been imagined just a few years ago.

In this report, we first show how the changing nature of the world economy makes it necessary not simply to reverse the decline in performance of the schools to which the first round of reform was addressed, but to reach far higher standards than any before. Second, we describe changes in the demography of the teaching force that threaten to wipe out all the gains made thus far. Third, we assert that only by having the finest teachers obtainable can the country address the problem it faces. Last, we lay out a strategy for transforming teaching and the structure of schools and education policy to reach that objective.

A Changing World Economy

Three years ago, the country was in the grip of the most severe recession since the Great Depression. While most Americans were deeply concerned about our economic prospects, and were persuaded that the economy could not prosper as long as the quality of education continued to decline, few perceived that the world economy was in the midst of a profound transformation, one that demands a new understanding of the education standards necessary to create the kind of high-wage work force that can compete in a global economy.

Not long ago, domestic producers of electronic appliances complained that the Japanese were able to undercut them with the use of low-paid workers. Later, many of these

"Our ability to compete in world markets is eroding. Growth in U.S. productivity lags far behind that of our foreign competitors. . . . Our world leadership is at stake, and so is our ability to provide for our people the standard of living and opportunities to which they aspire."

Global Competition: The New Reality, *The Report of the President's Commission on Industrial Competitiveness, 1985*

producers, along with many distributors and retailers, stopped complaining and contracted with low-cost producers in Japan for parts and finished products. It was widely assumed that America could continue to advance economically by producing the knowledge others would need to do the low-wage, low-skill work of actual production.

At a modern factory outside Seoul, Korean workers produce home video recorders sold under many brand names in the American market. They work seven days a week (with two days off a year), twelve hours a day. They earn $3,000 a year. Though the American market for home video recorders is big, profitable and growing, none of the machines sold here is produced in the U.S. We cannot, nor wish to, compete with these Korean workers on their own terms.

Now the Japanese are looking over their shoulders at Korea which is increasingly able to produce highly standardized goods at costs below those of the Japanese. The Japanese now realize that their continued economic progress depends on the production of goods and services incorporating state-of-the-art science and technology, an area in which the Koreans are not yet as good. So the Japanese are concentrating not just on superior manufacturing methods, an important factor in their success thus far, but on producing the knowledge needed to advance the state of the art, and incorporating that knowledge as efficiently as possible into production of new goods and services. It should come as no surprise that, just as we used to subcontract with the Japanese for the production of goods requiring little skill, the Japanese are now sub-

contracting with Korea and other Pacific nations.

These other countries are not likely to be long content with their assigned role as provider of the muscle, while others provide the brains. A short time ago an American executive of a firm that had just located a manufacturing plant in Singapore was told by a high government official: "You came because of our cheap labor and low taxes. You will stay because of the quality of our labor force."

We focus on America's economic relations with the Far East only to illustrate the mechanisms of a worldwide economic transformation. Advancing technology and the changing terms of international trade are remolding the basic structure of international economic competition. Both technology and capital now move across international borders with unprecedented ease and speed, seeking the lowest cost structures available for actual production. Products made and services rendered in the far corners of the earth can now be transported at very low cost to the world's largest markets. In those cases in which products and services can be produced by people with low skills who are willing to work hard for relatively low wages, the technology and capital will move to their doorstep. By low skills, we mean here the "basic skills" of minimum competence with written words and numbers, skills now possessed by many peoples of the world.

These developments challenge the most basic premises of the American economic system. This country developed the world's most productive economy in part by mass production techniques that made it possible to employ workers with modest skills to turn out high quality, inexpensive products in great volume. The economic benefits were passed on to workers in the form of rising wages, which they used to create a steadily expanding market for the goods and services they produced.

The key was the machinery. Very expensive machines were designed so as to reduce to a minimum the skills needed to operate them. Many skilled craftworkers were required, of course, but most jobs could be performed by unskilled and semi-skilled workers. The cost of the machines could be justified on the basis of the enormous market for the goods they produced, so the cost for each finished unit was very low. This is precisely the area in which we are today being beaten, because the same machinery is now available to others who are willing to work much longer hours than we are, at much lower wages, and markets are no longer national but worldwide. These new basic industry and mass production workers, like the turn-of-the-century American immigrant, are willing to work very hard because they see an opportunity to better themselves and the lives of their children.

If America wants to compete on the same terms as it did in the past — making the most of the workers with low skill levels — then it must accept prevailing world wage levels for low-skilled and semi-skilled labor. That is, we must be prepared for a massive decline in our standard of living. The alternative is to revise our view of the role of the worker in the economy. In the future, high-wage level societies will be those whose economies are based on the use on a wide scale of very highly skilled workers, backed up by the most advanced technologies available.

Some of America's premier firms operate on precisely such principles. There will always be enough highly educated people to meet their needs. But a handful of firms cannot sustain the American standard of living. If it is to be sustained, most of American business will have to emulate them, and their ability to do so will depend in part on a vast upgrading of the American work force.

While it is easy to move capital and technology, it is exceedingly difficult to create and sustain the conditions under which very large numbers of people become and remain well educated. When they are well educated, they more than pay for their high salaries by adding more to the value of the products they create and the services they offer than less skilled workers can possibly match. Investment in people requires far greater lead time than investment in machinery. Countries that fail to invest enough, or in time, will find the costs — sluggish productivity growth, joblessness, and declining real income — very high.

Concern over the quality of education in this country has been expressed in repeated warnings from the Education Commission of the States' Task Force on Education and Economic Growth, the President's Commission on Industrial Competitiveness, the National Alliance of Business and others. Yet we believe most Americans still do not fully

"Adam Smith, in The Wealth of Nations, *in 1776 pointed out that the wealth of nations was very much determined by the quality of its work force. Human resources provide the basis of productivity and productivity growth . . . . Without a literate, skilled, healthy, and motivated labor force, capital and technology cannot create a productive environment."*

Productivity Growth: A Better Life for America, *A Report to the President of the United States,* **White House Conference on Productivity, 1984**

"If only to keep and improve on the slim competitive edge we still retain in world markets, we must dedicate ourselves to the reform of our educational system . . ."

A Nation at Risk, *The National Commission on Excellence in Education,* **1983**

". . . it is our judgment that a high general level of education is perhaps the most important key to economic growth."

Action for Excellence, *Task Force on Education and the Economy, Education Commission of the States,* **1983**

"No sector [of the economy] can afford a growing underclass that cannot get or keep jobs . . . ."

Employment Policies: Looking to the Year 2000, *National Alliance of Business, 1986*

"The most fundamental requirement for a democracy is an educated citizenry capable of informed judgment on public issues. Participation in self-governance will require a higher standard of scientific literacy, a deeper understanding of history, and a greater capacity to think critically."

Who Will Teach Our Children? A Strategy for Improving California's Schools, *The Report of the California Commission on the Teaching Profession, 1985*

understand the gravity of the situation just described. Much of the rhetoric of the recent education reform movement has been couched in the language of decline, suggesting that standards have slipped, that the education system has grown lax and needs to return to some earlier performance standard to succeed. Our view is very different. We do not believe the educational system needs repairing; we believe it must be rebuilt to match the drastic change needed in our economy if we are to prepare our children for productive lives in the 21st century. It is no exaggeration to suggest that America must now provide to the many the same quality of education presently reserved for the fortunate few. The cost of not doing so will be a steady erosion in the American standard of living.

But even if by some economic miracle this country could remain competitive without rebuilding our education system, we must do so for other compelling reasons: equal opportunity for all our children and preservation of an informed population capable of self-government — a citizenry with a shared sense of democracy and a vision of our potential as a nation.

Those Left Out

This Task Force rejects the view that America must choose between quality and equity in education policy. It cannot afford to do so. The country must have both.

As the world economy changes shape, it would be fatal to assume that America can succeed if only a portion of our schoolchildren succeed. By the year 2000,

one out of every three Americans will be a member of a minority group. At present, one out of four American children is born into poverty, and the rate is increasing. While it was once possible for people to succeed in this society if they were simply willing to work hard, it is increasingly difficult for the poorly educated to find jobs. A growing number of permanently unemployed people seriously strains our social fabric. A heavily technology-based economy will be unable to invest vast sums to maintain people who cannot contribute to the nation's productivity. American business already spends billions of dollars a year retraining people who arrive at the workplace with inadequate education.

Another demographic change demands attention: the proportion of the population in the prime working years will decline steadily in the years ahead. Yet, this smaller working-age group will have to support a growing number of those who have retired from the work force. This makes it imperative that all those who are able to work make the maximum contribution to the economic well-being of the whole population.

Requirements of Democracy

We stress the relationship between education and the economy to drive home the economic costs of inadequate education. But we reject the view that preparation for work should be the only, or even the most important, goal of education. From the first days of the Republic, education has been recognized as the foundation of a democratic society for the nation and the individual alike. A passive electorate that derives much of its knowledge from television is too easily manipulated. School must provide a deeper understanding necessary for a self-governing citizenry. It must provide access to a shared cultural and intellectual heritage if it is to bind its citizens together in a commonweal. It certainly must enable the citizens of this country to make informed judgments about the complex issues and events that characterize life in advanced economies at the end of the 20th century. The cost of not doing so may well be the gradual erosion of our democratic birthright.

Learning in a Knowledge-Based Economy

Much of our system of elementary and secondary education evolved in the context of an economy based on mass production. It emphasized development of the routinized skills necessary for routinized work. A whole administrative system grew up to specify what routine skills were needed, including methods of student testing which are particularly well suited to the measurement of discrete, routine skills. These are skills that are now called "basic," the fundamentals of computation, the reading of straightforward texts, and the ability to recite the basic principles of democratic government. Teachers were engaged to convey these routine skills to students, based on texts written by others. A large bureaucracy emerged that tried to make this system work as smoothly as possible. The design of the bureaucracy was modeled on the factories in which many of the school graduates would work.

Now, many other countries, emulating this system, have large work forces whose mastery of routine skills equals or exceeds our own. Many of these countries are now in a position to compete in industries based on the use of large numbers of low-skill workers. These are the countries beating us at our own game.

As our system of secondary education evolved, provision of the practical skills required to pursue a vocation were emphasized for those not going to college. Despite periodic pressures for high intellectual standards in the curriculum for the college-bound, the curriculum largely reflects a smorgasbord of topics designed to keep students in school and off the streets.

It is not surprising that employers complain that graduates of such schools (and often graduates of colleges, too) find it hard to do the increasingly complex work required of them. They do not learn easily on the job, are unable to read complicated material, evaluate or make complex arguments, write well, or apply quantitative concepts and methods to unfamiliar problems.

The country is in a trap of our own making. Not all of our children actually master the basic skills. America has a serious functional literacy problem that must be corrected. However, as we seek to regain former levels of performance, we use the old measures to assess progress against the old goals. Over the last few years, many schools have demonstrated significant gains in student performance on standardized test scores and other measures of basic competence. But, at the same time, too many students lack the ability to reason and perform complex, nonroutine intellectual tasks. We are doing better

"Technological change and global competition make it imperative to equip students in public schools with skills that go beyond the 'basics.'"

Action for Excellence, *Task Force on Education for Economic Growth, Education Commission of the States, 1983*

At a time when economic growth is increasingly dependent on mastery of science and technology, U.S. eighth graders' knowledge and understanding of mathematics is below that of most of their counterparts in other industrialized countries.

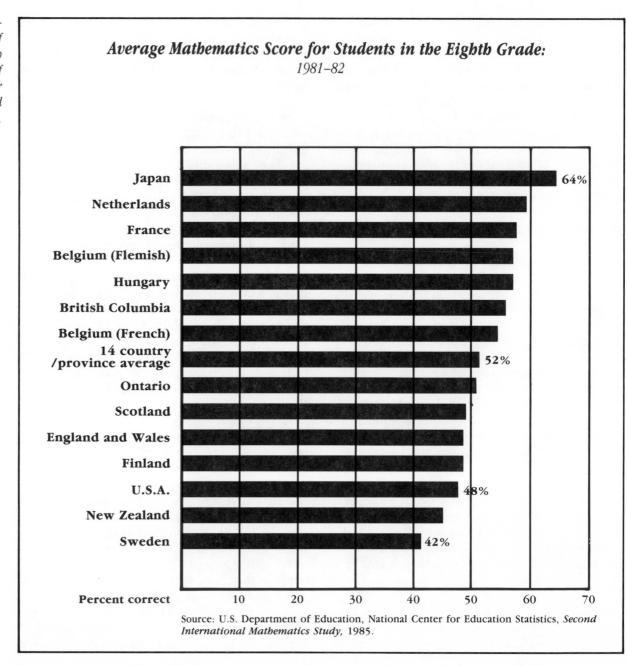

Average Mathematics Score for Students in the Eighth Grade:
1981–82

Japan	64%
Netherlands	
France	
Belgium (Flemish)	
Hungary	
British Columbia	
Belgium (French)	
14 country/province average	52%
Ontario	
Scotland	
England and Wales	
Finland	
U.S.A.	48%
New Zealand	
Sweden	42%

Percent correct   10   20   30   40   50   60   70

Source: U.S. Department of Education, National Center for Education Statistics, *Second International Mathematics Study,* 1985.

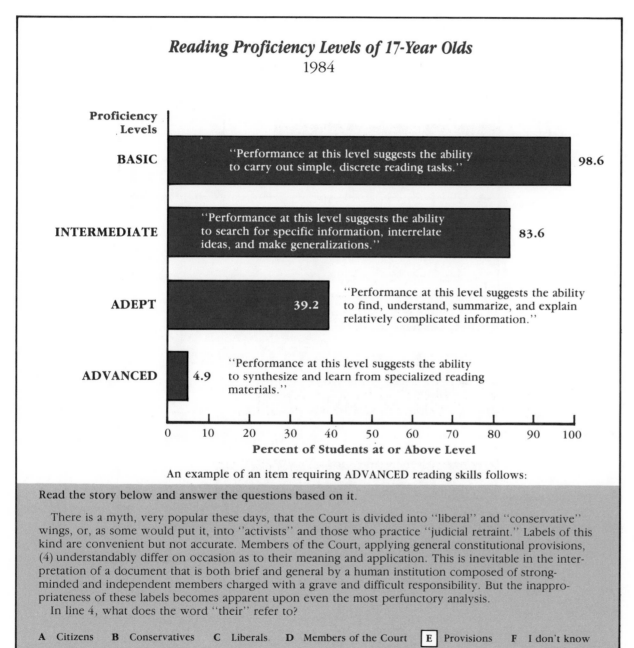

Reading Proficiency Levels of 17-Year Olds
1984

Proficiency Levels

BASIC — "Performance at this level suggests the ability to carry out simple, discrete reading tasks." — 98.6

INTERMEDIATE — "Performance at this level suggests the ability to search for specific information, interrelate ideas, and make generalizations." — 83.6

ADEPT — 39.2 — "Performance at this level suggests the ability to find, understand, summarize, and explain relatively complicated information."

ADVANCED — 4.9 — "Performance at this level suggests the ability to synthesize and learn from specialized reading materials."

0 10 20 30 40 50 60 70 80 90 100

Percent of Students at or Above Level

An example of an item requiring ADVANCED reading skills follows:

Read the story below and answer the questions based on it.

There is a myth, very popular these days, that the Court is divided into "liberal" and "conservative" wings, or, as some would put it, into "activists" and those who practice "judicial retraint." Labels of this kind are convenient but not accurate. Members of the Court, applying general constitutional provisions, (4) understandably differ on occasion as to their meaning and application. This is inevitable in the interpretation of a document that is both brief and general by a human institution composed of strong-minded and independent members charged with a grave and difficult responsibility. But the inappropriateness of these labels becomes apparent upon even the most perfunctory analysis.

In line 4, what does the word "their" refer to?

A Citizens **B** Conservatives **C** Liberals **D** Members of the Court **E** Provisions **F** I don't know

While young people leaving high school generally have good command of the mechanics of reading, the proportion able to analyze and explain more complicated material is very low.

"The world is moving into a technological-information age in which full participation in education, science, business, industry, and the professions requires increasing levels of literacy. What was a satisfactory level of literacy in 1950 probably will be marginal by the year 2000."
Becoming a Nation of Readers, *Commission on Reading,* **National Academy of Education, 1985**

Source: Educational Testing Service, National Assessment of Educational Progress, *The Reading Report Card: Progress Toward Excellence in Our Schools,* 1985.

In every mathematics category in which eighth grade students were examined, the performance of U.S. students was inferior to that of Japanese students—sometimes by very substantial amounts.

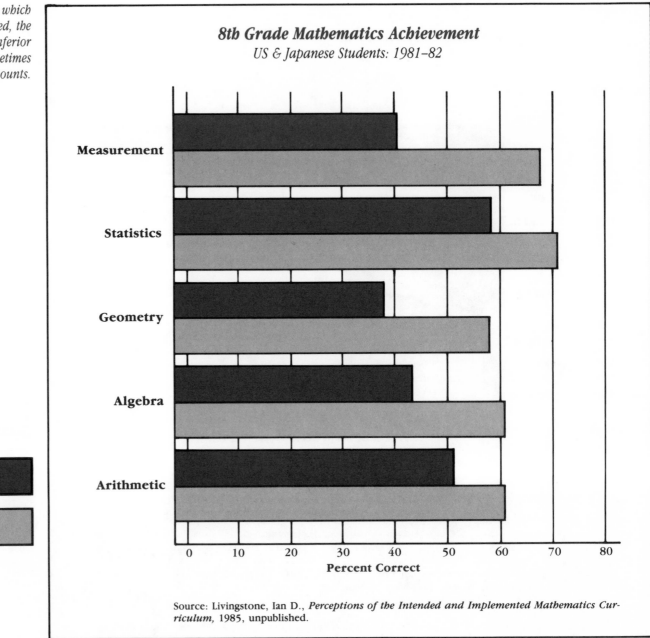

8th Grade Mathematics Achievement
US & Japanese Students: 1981–82

Measurement

Statistics

Geometry

Algebra

Arithmetic

United States

Japan

Percent Correct

0   10   20   30   40   50   60   70   80

Source: Livingstone, Ian D., *Perceptions of the Intended and Implemented Mathematics Curriculum,* 1985, unpublished.

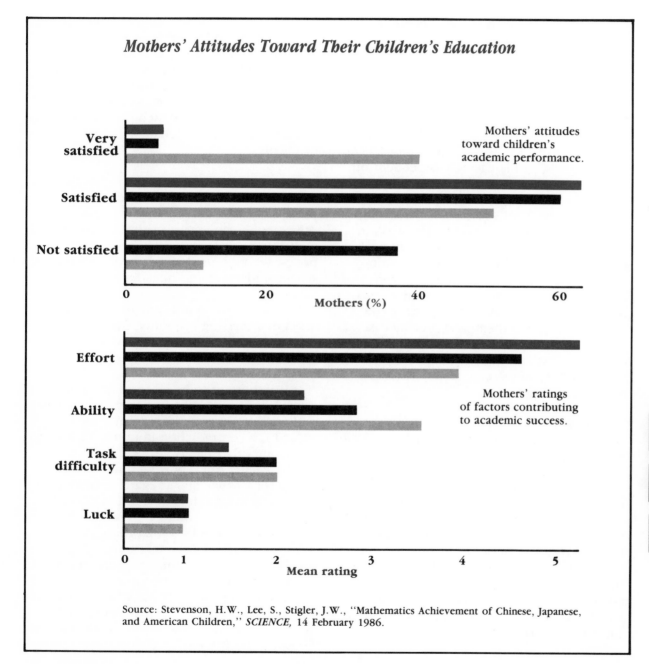

Mothers' Attitudes Toward Their Children's Education

Mothers' attitudes toward children's academic performance.

Very satisfied

Satisfied

Not satisfied

Mothers (%)

Mothers' ratings of factors contributing to academic success.

Effort

Ability

Task difficulty

Luck

Mean rating

Japan

Taiwan

U.S.

Source: Stevenson, H.W., Lee, S., Stigler, J.W., "Mathematics Achievement of Chinese, Japanese, and American Children," *SCIENCE*, 14 February 1986.

A study of elementary school children in metropolitan areas in Japan, Taiwan and the U.S. found that, although U.S. students performance in mathematics falls way below that of their counterparts in Japan and Taiwan, U.S. mothers seem well satisfied with their children's performance. Japanese and Taiwanese mothers in explaining success in schools apparently place more emphasis on "effort" than on "ability." For American mothers, it is just the opposite.

on the old goals, often at the expense of making progress on the goals that count the most. Because we have defined the problem of the schools in terms of decline from earlier standards, we have unwittingly chosen to face backwards when it is essential that we face forward.

The skills needed now are not routine. Our economy will be increasingly dependent on people who have a good intuitive grasp of the ways in which all kinds of physical and social systems work. They must possess a feeling for mathematical concepts and the ways in which they can be applied to difficult problems, an ability to see patterns of meaning where others see only confusion; a cultivated creativity that leads them to new problems, new products and new services before their competitors get to them; and, in may cases, the ability to work with other people in complex organizational environments where work groups must decide for themselves how to get the job done.

Such people will have the need and the ability to learn all the time, as the knowledge required to do their work twists and turns with new challenges and the progress of science and technology. They will not come to the workplace knowing all they have to know, but knowing how to figure out what they need to know, where to get it, and how to make meaning out of it. Even more important, if this country is to remain true to itself, our children should grow up to be humane and caring people, imbued with a set of values that enables them to use their skills in the service of the highest goals of the larger society.

They will, of course, have to have a basic stock of facts and know how to carry out basic procedures, but it will be essential for them to understand how those facts were derived and why those procedures work. They will spend a lifetime deciding which facts are relevant and which procedures will work for a constantly changing array of problems.

We are describing people who have the tools they need to think for themselves, people who can act independently and with others, who can render critical judgment and contribute constructively to many enterprises, whose knowledge is wide-ranging and whose understanding runs deep.

Such people will not only be the foundation of a thriving economy, they will be effective citizens. They are essential to our future.

It is important to be clear on one point. A knowledge-based economy in which learning and real intellectual effort are not highly valued is a contradiction in terms. Visitors to Japan and other newly successful countries on the Pacific rim report an omnivorous desire for knowledge, a regard for learning, and a belief that effort devoted to education will be rewarded. Some observers of the economic scene believe that these qualities account for Japan's economic success as much or more than others that are much more widely offered. The same qualities can be observed in many recent Asian immigrants to this country whose disproportionate success in our schools is a matter of record. The European tradition of intellectual rigor in the schools also persists. In our country, by contrast, real intellectual effort in schools is not often demanded by parents and is generally frowned upon by students' peers.

Success, then, depends on the whole society coming to place a much higher value not just on schooling but on learning. This demands a redefinition of the purposes of schooling, one that goes way beyond the inculcation of routine skills and the acquisition of a stock of facts. An economy based on people who think for a living requires schools dedicated to the creation of environments in which students become very adept at thinking for themselves, places where they master the art of learning and acquire a strong taste for it.

Our argument, then, is simple. If our standard of living is to be maintained, if the growth of a permanent underclass is to be averted, if democracy is to function effectively into the next century, our schools must graduate the vast majority of their students with achievement levels long thought possible for only the privileged few. The American mass education system, designed in the early part of the century for a mass-production economy, will not succeed unless it not only raises but redefines the essential standards of excellence and strives to make quality and equality of opportunity compatible with each other.

The Challenge

The Challenge

The Crucial Function of the Teacher

The students just described must be active learners, busily engaged in the process of bringing new knowledge and new ways of knowing to bear on a widening range of increasingly difficult problems. The focus of schooling must shift from teaching to learning, from the passive acquisition of facts and routines to the active application of ideas to problems. That transition makes the role of the teacher more important, not less.

It takes only a slight shift of perspective to see why this is so. With minor changes in language, the description we gave above of the students we need to develop can be reframed to describe the kinds of teachers needed to support the learning of those students:

Teachers should have a good grasp of the ways in which all kinds of physical and social systems work; a feeling for what data are and the uses to which they can be put, an ability to help students see patterns of meaning where others see only confusion; an ability to foster genuine creativity in students; and the ability to work with other people in work groups that decide for themselves how to get the job done. They must be able to learn all the time, as the knowledge required to do their work twists and turns with new challenges and the progress of science and technology. Teachers will not come to the school knowing all they have to know, but knowing how to figure out what they need to know, where to get

it, and how to help others make meaning out of it.

Teachers must think for themselves if they are to help others think for themselves, be able to act independently and collaborate with others, and render critical judgment. They must be people whose knowledge is wide-ranging and whose understanding runs deep.

We are describing people of substantial intellectual accomplishment. More than that, they are people who can communicate what they know to others, stimulate students to strive toward the same levels of accomplishment, and create environments in which young people not only get a taste for learning but build a base upon which they will continue to learn and apply what they know to the lives they go on to lead.

In schools where students are expected to master routine skills and acquire routine knowledge, the necessary skills and knowledge can, to a degree, be packaged in texts and teachers can be trained to deliver the material in the text to the students with reasonable efficiency. But a much higher order of skills is required to prepare students for the unexpected, the non-routine world they will face in the future. And a still higher order of skills is required to accomplish that task for the growing body of students whose environment outside the school does not support the kind of intellectual effort we have in mind.

"It is traditional wisdom in the business world that a corporation is only as good as the people it employs. Similarly, our schools can be no better than the teachers who staff them."

Investing in Our Children: Business and the Public Schools, *Committee for Economic Development, 1985*

"The new economy in Texas is an education-driven economy. We're looking for the intellectual fuel to compete in the information age. Originally, cotton farmers and cattle drivers were the source of the state's economic power. Then in 1901 at Spindletop the oil age came into being. Wildcatters suddenly became our most admired leaders, and they've taken us through most of the 20th century. But we can't take oil for granted anymore. Teachers and well-trained minds are now being called upon to lead the way. And like the venture capital it takes to build a new enterprise, their intellectual capital is the feed-stock of the new economy."

Governor Mark White
Texas

People with these characteristics are among the most sought after in our whole society. They staff the upper ranges of our most important institutions. We cannot hope to bring the mass of our citizens up to the standards we have proposed unless such people are available in large numbers to teach our children. Textbooks cannot do it. Principals cannot do it. Directives from state authorities cannot do it. Only the people with whom the students come in contact every day can do it.

Though many people have vital roles to play, only the teachers can finally accomplish the agenda we have just laid out.

The Second Wave of Reform

We have already described the objectives and accomplishments of the wave of education reform that has been underway during the last few years. In the effort to reverse the perceived decline of the last decade or more, many courageous actions have been taken and much of value has been achieved.

But some heavy prices have been paid. Many of the best people now staffing our schools, people who meet the requirements we have just laid out, are immensely frustrated — to the point of cynicism.

They see little change in the things that matter most to them, few policy developments that would enable them to meet the needs that have just been described. They see the bureaucratic structure within which they work becoming even more rigid, and the opportunities for exercising professional judgment becoming even more limited.

Increasingly, they believe that teachers are being made to pay the price for reform, and many do not believe that the current conception of reform will lead to real gains for students.

Reasonable people can differ as to the merits of these charges, but it is certainly true that real reform cannot be accomplished despite teachers. It will only come with their active participation. There is a real danger now of political gridlock, a situation in which those who would improve the schools from the outside are met by teachers on the inside who, because they distrust policymakers' motives and disapprove of their methods, will prevent further progress.

This impasse does not merely represent a clash of wills and interests. Underlying it is the reality that what must be done cannot be done within the constraints imposed by the system of public education that has been in place for many decades. A fundamental redesign of that system is needed, a redesign that will make it possible for those who would reform from the outside and those who would do so from the inside to make common cause. To see why this is so, it is necessary to describe the current condition of teachers and of teaching.

The Teacher Shortage

The challenge we have described comes at a time of extraordinary opportunity and great difficulty: a turning point in the national market for teachers. After years of teacher surplus, in 1985 jobs and job seekers were roughly in balance. For at least the next 10

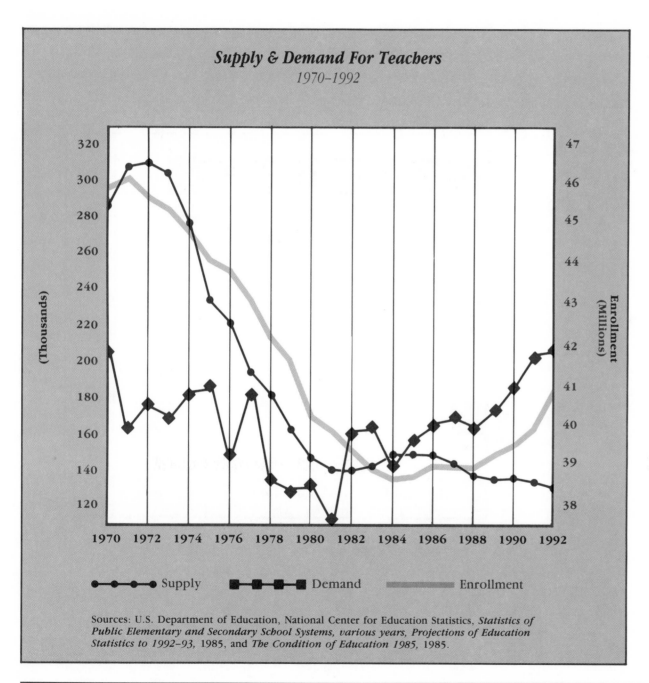

Supply & Demand For Teachers
1970–1992

Unless teaching as a career changes, in the years to come there will be a growing gap between teacher supply and demand, according to quite conservative projections.

(Thousands)

Enrollment (Millions)

●─●─● Supply   ■─■─■ Demand   ▬▬▬ Enrollment

Sources: U.S. Department of Education, National Center for Education Statistics, *Statistics of Public Elementary and Secondary School Systems, various years, Projections of Education Statistics to 1992–93,* 1985, and *The Condition of Education 1985,* 1985.

College students contemplating a career in teaching are being drawn to a greater extent than in the recent past from high school programs not designed to prepare students for college.

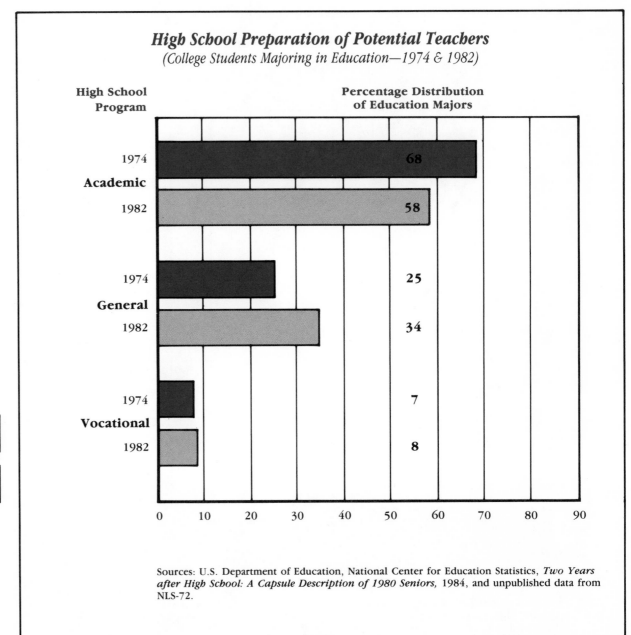

High School Preparation of Potential Teachers
(College Students Majoring in Education—1974 & 1982)

High School Program / **Percentage Distribution of Education Majors**

Academic
- 1974: 68
- 1982: 58

General
- 1974: 25
- 1982: 34

Vocational
- 1974: 7
- 1982: 8

1974 ■
1982 ▨

Sources: U.S. Department of Education, National Center for Education Statistics, *Two Years after High School: A Capsule Description of 1980 Seniors,* 1984, and unpublished data from NLS-72.

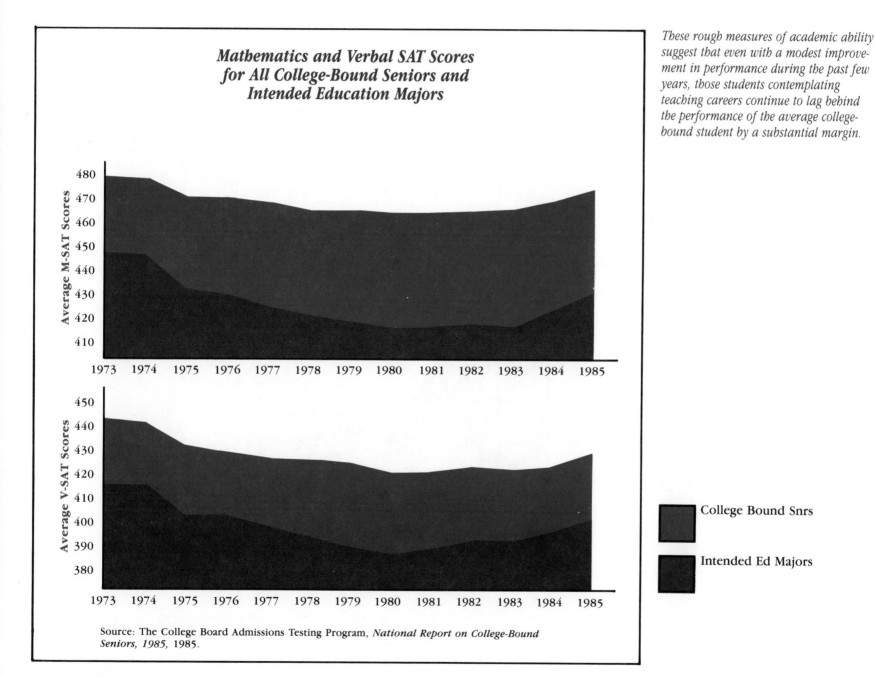

Mathematics and Verbal SAT Scores
for All College-Bound Seniors and
Intended Education Majors

These rough measures of academic ability suggest that even with a modest improvement in performance during the past few years, those students contemplating teaching careers continue to lag behind the performance of the average college-bound student by a substantial margin.

College Bound Snrs

Intended Ed Majors

Source: The College Board Admissions Testing Program, *National Report on College-Bound Seniors, 1985,* 1985.

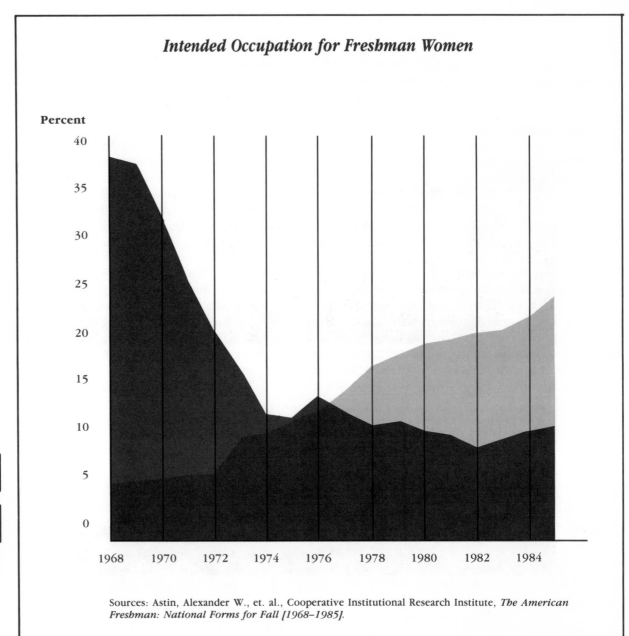

Intended Occupation for Freshman Women

Percent

Education

Business

Sources: Astin, Alexander W., et. al., Cooperative Institutional Research Institute, *The American Freshman: National Forms for Fall [1968–1985].*

years, however, there will be more jobs than applicants.

The end of the "baby boom" meant that few new teachers were hired in the 1970s and some teachers, usually those with the least seniority, were dismissed. The average age of teachers rose as a consequence, and many are now near retirement. Between the 1976-77 school year and the 1983-84 school year, the number of teachers 34 years old or less fell from 53 percent of all teachers to 37 percent. In the same period, those with four years of experience or less fell from 27 percent to 8 percent, while the teachers with fifteen or more years in the classroom went from 27 percent to 44 percent of all teachers. Simply because of impending retirements, many school districts face a situation in which half of their teachers may have to be replaced in the next three or four years.

There is another reason for increasing demand for teachers. The children of the children of the "baby boom" are now entering school.

Thus, we can anticipate a steep increase in the annual rate new teachers must be hired: from 115,000 new teachers in 1981 to 215,000 in 1992, by conservative estimates. Between 1986 and 1992, 1.3 million new teachers will be hired.

Several developments make it unlikely that the labor market alone will resolve these difficulties.

Although the proportion of entering college freshmen declaring an interest in a teaching career increased during the last three years from a low of 4.7 percent to 6.2 percent, this followed a fourteen-year period during which such interest plummeted by 80 percent. To the extent that the drop in supply was due to the fall in demand for teachers, we can expect that supply will increase to meet rising demand.

But the fall in supply was also due to a development that increasing demand will not remedy. Many more professional opportunities are open to able young women and minorities. College educated women who until recently had a choice of becoming a secretary, nurse or teacher can now, like the members of minority groups, choose for the first time from a great array of attractive possibilities. Many of the most accomplished teachers who are now in our schools have told interviewers that they would not choose teaching if they were beginning their careers anew.

Increasing demand is in fact swelling enrollments in teacher education institutions. But, with an estimated 23 percent of each college graduating class required to meet the need for teachers projected for the early 1990s, the recent gains of about one-half of one percent a year will not suffice.

Numbers are not the only problem. Though average Scholastic Aptitude Test scores of high school seniors intending to major in education have risen in the last two years, this slight gain follows a period of over 10 years during which the scores of prospective teachers declined at a faster pace than that experienced by all college-bound students. A wide gap remains between prospective teachers and all other college-bound seniors. Almost half of the students enrolling in teacher education come from non-academic high school programs, that is from general and vocational programs not intended to prepare students for college.

Yet another factor has widespread educational implications: growing numbers of disadvantaged students — from low-income families, non-English speaking backgrounds, and single-parent households. All youngsters need teachers with a much more sophisticated and complete understanding of their subjects, but the need of these children is greatest. These children, many of them the product of generations of poverty, find little in their environment outside of school that matches the affluent youngsters' push for academic success and the belief that it will pay off.

These students need more help than conventional teacher ratios permit. As the proportion of these students increases, the number of teachers required grows faster than school enrollment.

The proportion of minority students is also increasing. At the same time, the proportion of minority teachers is declining. Schools should be staffed by teachers who reflect the diversity of the nation's racial and cultural heritage. We cannot tolerate a future in which both white and minority children are confronted with almost exclusively white authority figures in the schools.

Leaving aside for the moment the need to improve school performance greatly, the demographic realities just described alone pose an impressive problem for education policymakers. Taken together, a steep increase in demand for teachers, a particularly acute need for minority teachers, and a declining supply of well-educated applicants constitute a challenge without precedent — an environment very different from the one in which the advances of the last three years have been made.

Seizing the Opportunity

Seizing the Opportunity

The situation just described has two faces. If the teacher shortage is dealt with as it usually has been in the past, districts will fill the empty slots by lowering their hiring standards. To make that strategy work now, the country will have to scrape the bottom of the barrel to find its teachers. Then, policymakers, whether they wish to or not, will be forced to dictate to these teachers what to do and how to do it. Under such conditions college-educated persons who have a choice of career will not elect to teach. These developments will bring the current education reform movement to a dead halt. If not adequately addressed, it will become absolutely impossible to achieve the much higher objectives we spelled out earlier. The consequence will be a decreasing standard of living for the nation as a whole, a growing underclass, and a citizenry unable to sustain its democratic traditions.

Alternatively, the country can conceive of the schools and the people in them as its most important investment, the key to our future. The very fact of the coming crisis in teaching presents a rare opportunity. The enormous turnover in the teaching force means that the decisions made in the next few years will have a striking impact on the composition of our teaching force for years to come, for better or worse. If the opportunity is seized now, the quality of our schools can be more quickly improved than at any time in the memory of most citizens.

Three challenges must be met at once if we are to obtain teachers of high intellectual ability, people with the kinds of skills that are in great demand in every sector of our society. The standards for entering teachers must be raised. Ways must be found to retain in our schools those teachers with the needed skills and to bring in others like them. And the structure of the system must be redesigned to take maximum advantage of those highly skilled teachers, so that the most efficient use is made of the additional funds required. We take each of these problems in turn.

Raising Standards

The time-honored response to teacher shortages is to lower standards for entry into the profession. But the only way to make sure the country gets the kind of teachers it needs is to raise them to levels never met before.

The effect of greatly raising standards in the face of a shortage would be electric. It would send a message to teachers and to young people deciding on a career that the country takes teachers and teaching seriously. This would only be true, of course, if the standards that are put in place reflect what a teacher needs to know and be able to do at a truly professional level of performance.

But it must be done fairly. Dramatic improvements for teachers are not likely unless teachers clearly meet higher standards of preparation and skill, but it is unfair to those now in place to change the rules under them all at once.

Raising standards will do no good if few applicants can meet the standards that are set. If the education of teachers is not greatly im-

"The present teacher training programs turn out persons who are not sufficiently equipped with the knowledge, the intellectual skills, or the developed understanding needed to guide and help the young in the course of study we have recommended."

The Paideia Proposal, *Mortimer Adler, 1982*

". . . every part of a teacher's education — from the liberal arts programs of the prospective teacher to the continuing education of the veteran — can be improved; even the best existing programs are not good enough."

A Call for Change in Teacher Education, National Commission for Excellence in Teacher Education, American Association of Colleges for Teacher Education, 1985

proved, the new teachers will be unable to perform up to the new expectations.

It might be said that our teachers are the victims of their own success. When the present system of teacher education was put in place some 50 years ago, its graduates enjoyed the respect they earned as a result of being among the best educated people in the community. In the intervening half century, arrangements for teacher education have changed little, but the general education level of the population as a whole has risen greatly, with the result that the respect teachers once enjoyed has diminished considerably. But the issue is not respect. The vital point is that the kinds of teachers needed in the years ahead will require far more rigorous preparation than all but a few receive now.

This is true both with respect to their general education as undergraduates and the development of their skills as teachers. Once again, teachers must be among the best educated people in their community.

Recruiting Highly Skilled Teachers

It will do little good to raise the standards for entry into the profession of teaching and greatly improve the professional preparation of teachers if nothing is done to make teaching a more attractive career. Few will make the effort to jump over a higher hurdle if there is little to be gained by doing so. Understanding the nature of this challenge requires an honest look at what it means to be a teacher.

Teaching, like nursing, is a feminized occupation. It took its current form in the 1930s and 1940s, when women were expected to subordinate their career aspirations to their childrearing responsibilities and their salary expectations to the man's role as breadwinner. Their work roles and the conditions under which many of them work more nearly resemble those of semiskilled workers on the assembly line rather than those of professionals.

It is hardly surprising in these circumstances that teachers' salaries rank with other feminized occupations at the bottom of all occupations requiring a college degree.

Even more to the point, the conditions under which teachers work are increasingly intolerable to people who qualify for jobs in the upper tiers of the American work force, the people who must now be attracted to teaching. Those people are, and tend to think of themselves, as professionals. Professional work is characterized by the assumption that the job of the professional is to bring special expertise and judgment to bear on the work at hand. Because their expertise and judgment is respected and they alone are presumed to have it, professionals enjoy a high degree of autonomy in carrying out their work. They define the standards used to evaluate the quality of work done, they decide what standards are used to judge the qualifications of professionals in their field, and they have a major voice in deciding what program of preparation is appropriate for professionals in their field.

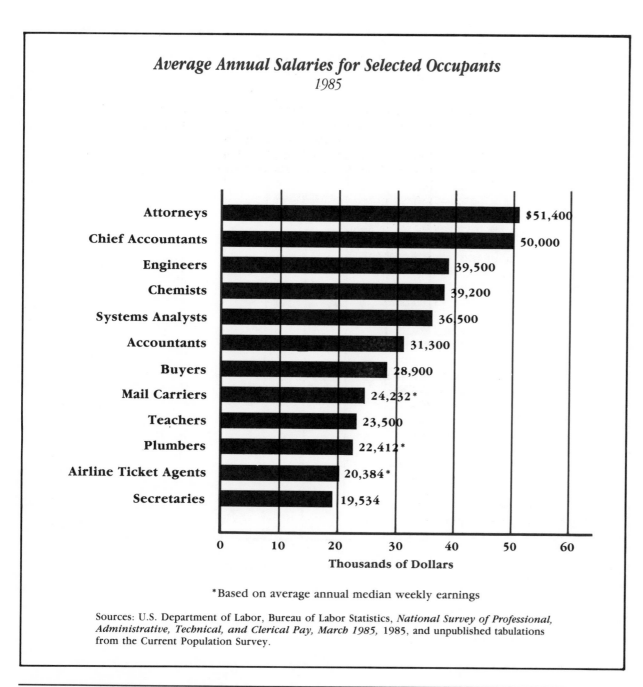

Average Annual Salaries for Selected Occupants
1985

Attorneys	$51,400
Chief Accountants	50,000
Engineers	39,500
Chemists	39,200
Systems Analysts	36,500
Accountants	31,300
Buyers	28,900
Mail Carriers	24,232*
Teachers	23,500
Plumbers	22,412*
Airline Ticket Agents	20,384*
Secretaries	19,534

0   10   20   30   40   50   60
Thousands of Dollars

*Based on average annual median weekly earnings

Sources: U.S. Department of Labor, Bureau of Labor Statistics, *National Survey of Professional, Administrative, Technical, and Clerical Pay, March 1985*, 1985, and unpublished tabulations from the Current Population Survey.

Teachers' salaries rank below those of most occupations requiring a college degree, and, in a number of instances, are no better than the salaries that can be earned in occupations requiring only a high school diploma.

"We believe that any call for comprehensive improvement in the public schools that does not recognize the need for additional resources is destined for failure."

Investing in our Children: Business and the Public Schools, *Committee for Economic Development, 1985*

At every point along the pipeline minority students drop out of the system at higher rates than non-minority students.

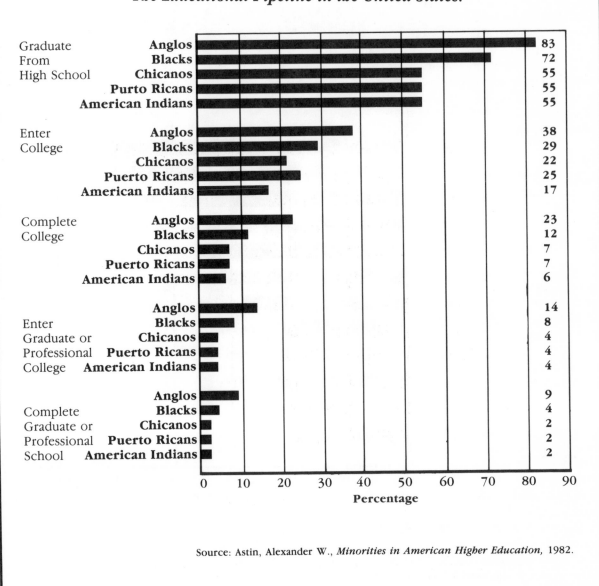

The Educational Pipeline in the United States.

		Percentage
Graduate From High School	Anglos	83
	Blacks	72
	Chicanos	55
	Purto Ricans	55
	American Indians	55
Enter College	Anglos	38
	Blacks	29
	Chicanos	22
	Puerto Ricans	25
	American Indians	17
Complete College	Anglos	23
	Blacks	12
	Chicanos	7
	Puerto Ricans	7
	American Indians	6
Enter Graduate or Professional College	Anglos	14
	Blacks	8
	Chicanos	4
	Puerto Ricans	4
	American Indians	4
Complete Graduate or Professional School	Anglos	9
	Blacks	4
	Chicanos	2
	Puerto Ricans	2
	American Indians	2

Source: Astin, Alexander W., *Minorities in American Higher Education,* 1982.

Seizing the Opportunity

Because professionals themselves are expected to have the expertise they need to do their work, organizations that employ professionals are not typically based on the authority of supervisors, but rather on collegial relationships among the professionals. This does not mean no one is in charge, but it does mean that people practicing their profession decide what is to be done and how it is to be done within the constraints imposed by the larger goals of the organization.

Work in such organizations is often challenging and fulfilling. A large body of research shows that it is these conditions of work, at least as much as the high salaries that typically accompany it, that attract our most able college graduates.

The conditions we have just described are rarely to be found in our schools. Teachers work in an environment suffused with bureaucracy. Rules made by others govern their behavior at every turn. Perceptive researchers have told us for years that teachers are treated as if they have no expertise worth having. The text and the scope-and-sequence of the curriculum define in detail what they are supposed to teach. Decisions made by curriculum supervisors, teacher training experts, outside consultants and authors of teachers' guides determine how a teacher is to teach. Teachers who choose to work together as professional colleagues must constantly fight the natural tendencies of a system based on very different principles. And an endless array of policies succeed in constraining the exercise of the teacher's independent judgment on almost every matter of moment.

There may be some who believe that all this is fully justified by what they perceive as teachers of inadequate ability. But the plain fact is that the many good teachers we have are being driven out of teaching by these conditions, and it will be impossible to attract many new people of real ability to teaching until these conditions are radically altered.

The cynicism of many teachers today is due to the fact that, despite the many worthwhile changes being made in education policy, they see little that would change the underlying conditions just described.

In a nutshell, recruiting the most able college graduates to teaching will require the schools to offer pay and conditions of work that are competitive with those to be found in other places where professional work is done. That means fundamental change in both the schools and the profession of teaching.

What we have just said applies to all teachers. There is a special problem with respect to minority teachers. The education available to minority and poor children is often lacking in quality compared to that offered to others. They drop out of the educational "pipeline" much faster than other children. The result is that obtaining adequate numbers of minority teachers requires more than making teaching an attractive career. There are simply not enough minority students graduating from college with strong academic records to meet the growing need for minority teachers. Only a massive effort to improve the education of minority and poor students from elementary school

"Many of the teachers in elementary schools are not qualified to teach mathematics and science for even 30 minutes a day. A significant fraction of our secondary school teachers are called upon to work in subjects for which they were never trained. Even the most seasoned and experienced veterans must deal with subjects that are in a state of constant change; no one can remain knowledgeable in science without constant refreshing."

Educating Americans for the 21st Century, *The National Science Board Commission on Precollege Education in Mathematics, Science and Technology, 1983*

"Improving American secondary education absolutely depends on improving the conditions of work and the respect for teachers.

". . . Hired hands own nothing, are told what to do, and have little stake in their enterprises. Teachers are often treated like hired hands. Not surprisingly, they often act like hired hands.

". . . Excellent schooling requires excellent teachers and principals. Excellent people have self-confidence and self-esteem and expect reasonable autonomy. Therefore, if we want excellent schools, we must give more power to the teachers and principals."

Horace's Compromise, *Theodore Sizer, 1984*

through graduate school will effectively address the problem.

The Structure of the Teaching Work Force and the Schools

As we noted earlier, professionals are a valuable resource in our society. It takes a lot of education and training to produce them and costs a lot of money to pay them. For that reason, most employers work hard at making the most of these professionals.

That is why professionals are typically supported by many other people who do the work they would otherwise have to do. The services of these other people come at lower cost, so it is more efficient to use them to perform such tasks than to have them performed by the professionals. For the same reasons, professionals also have available to them a host of machines and services that improve their efficiency in countless ways, from computers and copying machines to telephones and adequate work space. These services are not perquisites for professionals. They are regarded by employers as necessary investments, enabling the professionals on their staffs to reach the highest possible levels of accomplishment.

To take but one of many possible examples, architects typically have available the services of model builders and people to do their drafting, as well as clerks, receptionists and accountants. They rarely fail to meet a deadline because they run out of lead for drafting pencils, or paper for their copying machines. Most willingly invest in automated drafting and design equipment, because, ex-

pensive as these aids are, they cost less than the time expensive architects would otherwise have to spend, and they make it possible to render services to the client that would be intolerably expensive if provided by other means.

Not only do professionals typically have a range of support staff and services available, but they are usually organized so that the most able among them influence in many ways the work that others do, from broad policy direction to the development of staff members who might some day take on major responsibilities. This, too, is a matter of simple efficiency, making sure that the experience and skill embodied in these valuable people makes itself felt throughout the enterprise.

This is not the world of schools, not the world that teachers live in. Teachers spend between 10 percent and 50 percent of their time on non-instructional duties — everything from recording test scores to monitoring the halls, from doing lunchroom and playground duty to running the ditto machine. They are constantly running out of supplies, forced to use outdated texts, and make do with inadequate materials. Skilled support help is rarely available, nor the time to do the job right.

Highly skilled and experienced teachers are typically used no differently than the novice. The system rarely takes advantage of their expertise in ways that would make it available to less skilled members of the staff.

These are hard facts. They build a powerful case that Americans care more about providing adequate support staff and services to those who design the appliances we use, make television programs for our evening entertainment and engineer our roads, than to those who educate our children.

America's schools can, without doubt, greatly improve their performance. They will not do so unless they prove to be an attractive employment opportunity to some of the most able college graduates in the country. But the schools cannot realistically expect that all 2.3 million teachers will be the best and brightest the country has to offer. Education, like other professions, will have to structure itself so that it can make the very best use of a distribution of talent. That means reorganization, because the current "eggcrate" organization does not permit efficient shared use of highly skilled people, support services and equipment.

The Grounds for Optimism

Meeting these requirements implies far reaching changes in our schools and in education policy, changes we will make explicit below. There is every reason to be optimistic about the country meeting the challenge. A strong base has been laid in many states for the advances that must come next. There is a growing awareness that further progress is unlikely without fundamental changes in structure. In fact, we suspect that dramatic change may be easier to achieve than incremental change, given the growing frustration with political gridlock and the increasing awareness that the biggest impediment to progress is the nature of the system itself. While many polls show that Americans are relatively satisfied with their schools, they also show that voters would be willing to finance significant increases in school expenditures if they are persuaded that great improvements in performance will follow.

"I believe that...the principle of 'every tub on its own bottom,' or nearly on its own bottom, would go a long way toward developing schools that took care of their own business, rectified chronic problems, and communicated effectively with parents — characteristics of the more satisfying schools in our sample.

"... Further, I envision that, in time, those associated with schools would become increasingly creative in designing alternative programs of instruction — something not characteristic of the schools in our sample. And finally, I believe that the potential for developing an increased sense of ownership on the part of those associated with the local school would be vastly enhanced."

"Given the labor-intensive character of teaching, it simply is not economically feasible to pay attractive salaries to all who teach .... The alternative is a deliberate distinction among various assisting and apprentice roles, more highly paid career teachers, and ... head teachers."

A Place Called School, *John Goodlad,* *1984*

Schools for the 21st Century:
A Scenario

Schools for the 21st Century: A Scenario

This report is concerned with policy. But it is policy with a purpose, policy designed to create the schools we need. It is an old saw that a picture is worth a thousand words. In this section, we paint a picture of the kind of schools that might be common 10 or 15 years from now (when our preschoolers are graduating from high school) if the policies we propose are actually enacted. Our aim is to invite the reader to imagine with us what might be achieved if the country makes the necessary effort.

There is a danger in drawing such pictures. Concreteness has its drawbacks. People rightly want many different kinds of schools. Inevitably, some people who might agree with our recommendations will object to one or more features of the specific example we describe. Please bear in mind that we, too, want many different kinds of schools. The scenario that follows is but one way in which schools might evolve.

It is the year 2000. We are in a high school in a midwestern city serving children in a low income community. Most of the professional teaching staff have been Board certified. Many hold the Advanced Certificate issued by the Board. The professional teachers run the school with an Executive Committee of Lead Teachers in overall charge. There are many other people available to help the teachers, including paid teachers aides, technicians and clerical help; interns and residents working in the school as part of their professional teacher preparation programs; student tutors from the university, a few people on loan from nearby firms, and a retired person working as a volunteer tutor.

We begin our visit by talking with several eleventh graders about their work in history and government. Last year, the history teacher had the students study the muckrakers and the "good government" movement in the Progressive Era. They got a good grasp of the central issues at stake in those days. Earlier this year, many of those students served as interns in local government agencies. They prepared reports on their work that included some rather interesting analyses of the role of local government and the conflicts that arise. When they sat for their exam in government at the end of the semester, they evidently surprised some of the readers with their ability to bring a strong historical perspective to the way they framed and defended their views on the exam questions. They were asked to describe the advantages and disadvantages for various groups in the city of the bill now before the legislature to convert from the current strong mayor form of local government to a city manager form.

Most of these students did very well on the local government part of the state exams the next year even though some of the questions on the exam were on subjects they had not studied. With their strong historical perspective and firm understanding of the dynamics of city government and politics, they could figure out what kind of information they needed to answer the exam questions. They picked out the relevant facts very quickly from the data the examiners had supplied for the students. Because their analytical skills were pretty sharp they could sift through and interpret the information to come to a defensible — and often rather original — answer to the exam questions.

What was really exciting from these youngsters' point of view was what happened this morning when the political columnist in the major daily paper came over for a seminar. They were evidently able to convince him that he had misunderstood the real nature of a key issue in the recent election, and he had gone off saying that he was going to write a column on that point that would acknowledge their contribution. They could not wait until the column appeared in the paper. One of the students said with determination that he was going to study journalism in college and become a columnist, too. Another said she would not be content with reporting on politics, but was going to study political science and become a politician herself.

We decide to visit with these youngsters' social studies teacher, Dave Oxton, in his office. A Phi Beta Kappa graduate of the University of Chicago, he is full of pride in his students. Most come, he says, from low-income families. Their parents are not well educated and few expected their children to do well in school or go to college.

Dave, who is Black, grew up in a community very like the one he now teaches in. He describes how he and two other teachers have worked with these students and their families over the last 15 years. When they started out at the school, they sought out the leaders of several community based organizations and city agencies, and put together a plan for helping the teachers in the school to see the world as the students saw it, and to help the community based organizations and city agencies coordinate their programs more closely with one another and with the school.

Eventually, the local business community was drawn in. They made it clear to the school staff and the students what skills the students needed to get entry level jobs and promised that jobs would in fact be available to those students who met the standards, and wanted to go to work right out of high school.

Three nearby colleges and one university joined in, providing college students to tutor the youngsters, advisers to help them understand what was needed to go to college, and an intensive summer enrichment program to help them keep up with the school's demanding curriculum. As these youngsters began to believe in themselves and their ability to succeed academically, they found they could do as well as any students in the community. Their own success made believers out of the students in the lower schools.

One effort that made a surprisingly big difference — both for the high school students and the younger students — was the program in which the older students were trained to tutor the younger ones. When many of the older youngsters discovered how superficial their knowledge was when they tried to teach something they thought they knew, they made a real effort to master the material. They developed a real pride in their ability to help the younger students and many are going on to become teachers.

All of this, says Dave, is much easier to describe than it was to do. His background, and that of his colleagues, helped a lot. Dave's degree is in history. The two other teachers with whom he has worked closely have degrees in economics and psychology. Together, they had the skills they needed to analyze what was really going on in the community and in the lives of these students and their parents. They were able to draw on their undergraduate and graduate studies to get a perspective on the problems these students faced and on the techniques that might work to address those problems that would otherwise have been very hard to come by.

We have an hour before our appointment with Maria Lopez, the Lead Teacher elected by her peers as the head of the executive committee of the school. We duck into a lab room where 10 students are working, a few alone, others in small groups. Computer work stations are scattered about. A lab technician is working with some of the students.

One small group of students is developing a strategy for their full time, three-week project to assess the toxicity of the pollutants in an open sewer. They have to analyze the chemical and biological composition of the effluent, locate its source, and bring their results to the attention of the appropriate authorities. They are working on the project with the city's environmental agency, a local firm that specializes in the analysis of toxic materials, and their teachers of chemistry, biology and social studies. They know that all this work is intended to help them prepare for their statewide test in science, but they know also that their social studies teacher has designed the project so they will be well prepared for that part of the social studies examination that deals with students' grasp of conflicts in public policy.

Sarena Welsh, one of the students, does a computer search and comes up with some articles that might be used to build a candidate list of pollutants, and a second that lists standard computer-based analysis techniques for determining the presence of these pollutants in the effluent. Another student, Jim Howard, whose interests run more toward policy issues, searches the city data base to find the names of companies that have been cited over the last few years for violations of the state and local environmental laws. They know that their teachers can help them interpret the more technical language in these sources, but they want to go as far as they can on their own. Bill remembers that one of their instructors, who works part time at the local firm that is involved in the project, offered to loan some analysis equipment that the group can use with their school computers. He calls him to arrange for the use of the equipment next week. Sarena calls an assistant director of the environmental agency who agrees to give the team a briefing on the legal procedures involved in resolving environmental issues. Together they put together a work plan, knowing that their teachers will take it apart ruthlessly when they make their presentation in two days.

We cannot help but be impressed with the mastery of subjects displayed by these students, subjects that, until only a few years ago, were not typically taught until college or even later. What is even more impressive is that these students exhibit the healthy skepticism of inquiring minds, genuine creativity, and a real understanding of the conceptual underpinning of the subjects they have studied which they are able to apply to solving real problems.

There is half an hour left before our appointment with Maria Lopez. We drop in on a class in which there is a spirited debate going on. The teacher had asked the students to speculate about how Mark Twain would have written A Connecticut Yankee in King Arthur's Court *if he had written it toward the end of the 20th Century. The assignment called for some knowledge of the critical literature on the book itself, a good feel for the spirit of the times in which Mark Twain lived, and an analysis of the current American character and outlook. Each of the students has written a critical essay on the topic, and six have been selected to defend their positions before the rest of the class.*

The students know that their test in this course will be based not just on the knowledge of what others have said about a major work of literature, but also on their ability to come up with original analyses that make use of the critical methods they have studied, as well as what they know about American culture and technological development.

Sally Hubby, the teacher, majored as an undergraduate in American literature. She is supported in this course by an instructor who graduated with honors from Ball State University with a degree in American history. The instructor is working on his Master in Teaching degree at the university. This particular class is being conducted by the instructor, while the teacher works with a small group of students engaged in a special project. The two work really well together. Sally, who has an Advanced Certificate from the Board and holds down important leadership responsibilities in the school, has started to look for opportunities to involve the young instructor on several teachers' committees to give him an opportunity to take on additional responsibilities in stages.

On the way to Maria Lopez' office we pass the computer graphics lab. It is presided over by Martin Southworth, an engineer on the staff of Applied Infometrics, a local software engineering firm. Martin, we are told, is a specialist on the uses of computer based graphics and design tools. We learned that most of the students in the class are planning to go into various technical support roles in the local machine tool industry, but Martin takes particular pride in the fact that several young women in the school, after working in his lab, decided on pursuing engineering careers in college. He got them hooked on design work and then worked with the Lead Teachers in the math and science areas to make the courses in that area build on their enthusiasm for design.

The conversation with the chair of the executive committee gets off to a fast start. A question about the goals of the school produces an animated monologue that lasts almost half an hour. Maria Lopez describes how the professional teachers in the schools met with the parents over six months to come to an understanding about what they wanted for their children, how they then discussed state and local standards and objectives, and then came up with a plan for their school.

It was a tricky process. The teachers' plan had to address the state and local objectives for these students, and take into account what the parents wanted as well. But in the end, the objectives had to reflect what the teachers themselves thought they could and should accomplish for the students. If they set the objectives too low, they might be easily accomplished, but the teachers' bonuses would be commensurately low. Achievement of ambitious objectives would bring substantial rewards under their bonus plan, but none at all if they were not met. After long discussions with the district administrators, some objectives were set lower than the district had in mind, but others were set higher. Needless to say, the teachers were very interested in the year-end results that would be made public four weeks after the end of the spring term.

Other districts and other states, she said, used very different methods to provide incentives to the teachers for producing real gains for students. This method had been worked out through a process in which the teachers had been fully involved and with which they were comfortable, and that had produced real commitment on their part to the system. But it would not work at all, she observed, were it not for the fact that the teachers had the resources they need to provide an effective instructional environment for the students and the freedom to decide how those resources were used.

We have to break off the conversation to go to the weekly teachers' meeting.

The teachers' committee working on restructuring the school day gives a progress report. The Lead Teacher who chairs the committee, one of the most respected teachers in the school, begins by reminding everyone that the committee was created because the teachers needed more time to coach individual students, and thought too much time was being spent in lecture style classes. The committee lays out an approach that relies more heavily on the use of small seminar sessions run by instructors whose work is supervised by the professional teachers, freeing teachers for more time to work with individual students. The meeting gives its approval to the general approach, points out some problems, and sets a date for the next report.

Members of another committee bring in a plan for introducing advanced mathematics concepts at an earlier level than they now appear in the curriculum. They have been following a debate about the evolving techniques of mathematical modeling closely and are convinced that high school students can grasp the fundamentals of these techniques if they can be taught in the context of real applications. They have been working with some local firms that use the new approaches in their business, and offer an approach to instruction that involves seminar work at the school closely integrated with field work in the firms. Their report includes an incisive analysis of the conceptual problems students typically have in grasping the techniques and the pedagogical methods that can be used to overcome them. They note in passing that some recent immigrants seem to have particular difficulty in dealing with this material. One of the Lead Teachers who has become a recognized expert in the cultural background of these immigrant children points out that the native language of these students does not include words for key concepts. He suggests some journal articles that the committee might read to help them overcome the problem.

A Lead Teacher who heads a committee attempting to develop a curriculum to stimulate creative problem-solving behavior in students reports on the success of a trial approach based on the combined efforts of a poet from the community arts center and a science teacher. The students have come to see that there are many ways to frame problems and many ways to approach the solution of those problems. Their search for right answers has yielded to the insight that intuition plays a major role in science and structure plays an equally important role in poetry. It is too early to draw firm conclusions, she says, but the first round of student scores on the new state examinations in science and English seem to indicate that this approach might pay handsome dividends. The teachers agree to extend the experiment to other areas of the curriculum.

The meeting closes with a report from the school administrator hired by the teachers' executive committee last year. She has worked up a specification for specialized testing services, based on the technical information provided by the teachers with advanced training in psychometrics. The school district central office and the local office of a national firm have both submitted bids. After a short but heated debate, the teachers decide to award the contract to the school district, based on the great improvement in the district's technical staff and their ability to respond quickly to changing requirements.

After the meeting, we get another few minutes with Maria Lopez. In response to our questions, she acknowledges that the professional teachers on her staff spend more time deciding how the school is to run than they used to. But, despite this, they have no less time to devote to instruction than before, because there are many more people around to take care of all the things which used to occupy teachers that had nothing to do with instruction.

She leans across the table to make the main point. This school, she says, could never have accomplished what it has in the last few years without the Board-certified teachers it has. Their skill, commitment and drive are the school's biggest asset. When the state revised its education code 10 years ago to focus on holding teachers accountable for student performance, leaving them free to decide how the objectives were going to be achieved, she saw an enormous improvement in the morale of her best teachers and a rededication to teaching. The reorganization of the school soon followed, creating a very flexible approach to the use of all kinds of people now available to support the professional teachers. Over the years, the Lead Teachers have worked out subtle ways of guiding the development of the school without recreating the old bureaucratic methods. There is nothing she would rather do, Maria says, than teach.

But what matters most, she says, are the students. The improvement in their performance over the years has been nothing short of spectacular. Dropouts have all but disappeared. Using the state tests as a measure, the academic skills of those not going on to college right away are nearly as strong as those of the most able students in this inner city school a decade ago. The best students are performing at a level that is close to that of the top students in the state. The pride in her voice as she says all this is unmistakable.

This is not a utopian vision. There are schools in the United States whose staffs would recognize this description as being very like what they do now. But not many. And few indeed that serve less fortunate children. In the section that follows, we lay out a plan that we believe will make such schools common. It will not be easy to achieve, but it is an educationally sound, practical plan, one that is very much within the reach of possibility, as is the school we have just described.

The Plan

The Plan

A New Framework

Though the plan we recommend is complex, the goal is clear: a system in which school districts can offer the pay, autonomy and career opportunities necessary to attract to teaching highly qualified people who would otherwise take up other professional careers. In return, teachers would agree to higher standards for themselves and real accountability for student performance. This framework implies a transformation of the environment for teaching. School systems based on bureaucratic authority must be replaced by schools in which authority is grounded in the professional competence of the teacher, and where teachers work together as colleagues, constantly striving to improve their performance.

A plausible plan for producing this outcome must meet many criteria: the cost must be within reach; those who agree to the necessary changes must have something to gain; and the plan must hold out the promise that increased student performance will justify increased cost.

The plan draws heavily on analogies to professional work elsewhere. But we have been careful to avoid important problems associated with many other professions, including the cost pressure caused by limiting entry through the use of standards unrelated to the actual demands of the job, lack of accountability, and inhibitions on innovation.

The plan includes the following major elements:

- Create a National Board for Professional Teaching Standards, organized with a regional and state membership structure, to establish high standards for what teachers need to know and be able to do, and to certify teachers who meet that standard.

- Restructure schools to provide a professional environment for teachers, freeing them to decide how best to meet state and local goals for children while holding them accountable for student progress.

- Restructure the teaching force, and introduce a new category of Lead Teachers with the proven ability to provide active leadership in the redesign of the schools and in helping their colleagues to uphold high standards of learning and teaching.

- Require a bachelors degree in the arts and sciences as a prerequisite for the professional study of teaching.

- Develop a new professional curriculum in graduate schools of education leading to a Master in Teaching degree, based on systematic knowledge of teaching and including internships and residencies in the schools.

- Mobilize the nation's resources to prepare minority youngsters for teaching careers.

- Relate incentives for teachers to school-wide student performance, and provide schools with the technology, services and staff essential to teacher productivity.

- Make teachers' salaries and career oppor-

State and local policy makers should work with teachers to create schools that provide a professional environment for teaching.

1. Teachers should be provided with the discretion and autonomy that are the hallmarks of professional work. State and local governments should set clear goals for schools and greatly reduce bureaucratic regulation of school processes. Teachers should participate in the setting of goals for their school and be accountable for achieving agreed upon standards of performance.

2. Districts should foster collegial styles of decisionmaking and teaching in schools in which "Lead Teachers" play a central role. Lead Teachers in the future should hold advanced teacher's certificates from a new National Board for Professional Teaching Standards.

3. Teachers should be provided the support staff they need to be more effective and productive, and should be prepared to take responsibility for overseeing the work of additional staff with a range of skills and experience.

4. School districts should consider a variety of approaches to school leadership.

tunities competitive with those in other professions.

This is not a list of independent strategies. They constitute a whole. None will succeed unless all are implemented.

To see why this is so, one need only start with any element to see how it leads to the others.

Raising the quality of teacher preparation will not work by itself, since few people will go to the added expense and effort of a longer period of teacher preparation unless the career that is offered is at least as attractive as other professions requiring demanding preparation. But it is also true that raising teacher pay will not improve matters much if the people who are paid more are no better prepared for the work they do.

Giving teachers a greater voice in the decisions that affect the school will make teaching more attractive to good teachers who are already in our schools as well as people considering teaching as a career. However, policymakers are unlikely to give teachers more autonomy unless they are convinced that teachers have strong incentives to meet the goals set for students by the district and the state.

Conversely, teachers are not likely to be willing to be held accountable unless they have substantial control over the way their services are delivered to students.

Higher teacher pay is an absolute prerequisite to attracting — and keeping — the people

we want in teaching. But pay that is high enough is not likely to be forthcoming unless standards for teachers are high enough to justify the cost. It also works the other way around. Teachers are unlikely to reach for higher standards unless substantial raises in pay are provided.

If the standards are raised, there will be serious consequences for minority teachers unless a massive effort is made to improve the education of poor and minority students and attract substantial numbers to teaching. Improving their education, however, while a very important objective in its own right, will not result in substantial increases in the number of minority teachers unless teaching is made more attractive as a career.

The point has been made. Policymakers will be tempted to implement only those features of this plan that cost little in organizational trauma or dollars. That would inevitably defeat the purpose, because the result would be to leave in place the forces that make the current system work the way it does. It is the entire structure that needs an overhaul, not just a few components.

A Professional Environment for Teaching

One of the most attractive aspects of professional work is the way professionals are treated in the workplace. Professionals are presumed to know what they are doing, and are paid to exercise their judgment. Schools on the other hand operate as if consultants, school district experts, textbook authors, trainers, and distant officials possess more relevant expertise than the teachers in the schools. Bureaucratic management of schools proceeds from the view that teachers lack the talent or motivation to think for themselves. Properly staffed schools can only succeed if they operate on the principle that the essential resource is already inside the school: determined, intelligent and capable teachers. Such schools will be characterized by autonomy for the school as a whole and collegial relationships among its faculty.

Professional autonomy. Professional autonomy is the first requirement. If the schools are to compete successfully with medicine, architecture, and accounting for staff, then teachers will have to have comparable authority in making the key decisions about the services they render. Within the context of a limited set of clear goals for students set by state and local policymakers, teachers, working together, must be free to exercise their professional judgment as to the best way to achieve these goals. This means the ability to make — or at least to strongly influence — decisions concerning such things as the materials and instructional methods to be used, the staffing structure to be employed, the organization of the school day, the assignment of students, the consultants to be used, and the allocation of resources available to the school.

This autonomy will work only if the school staff work collaboratively, taking collective responsibility for student progress.

The School as a Collegium and the Role of Lead Teachers. In most professional organizations those who are most experienced and highly skilled play the lead role in guiding the activi-

ty of others. We propose that districts create positions for a group of such people, designated "Lead Teachers," in each school. They would be selected from among experienced teachers who are highly regarded by their colleagues and possess Advanced Teacher's Certificates from the National Board for Professional Teaching Standards (described in the next section of this Chapter). Their role would be to guide and influence the activity of others, ensuring that the skill and energy of their colleagues is drawn on as the organization improves its performance.

We do not envision Lead Teachers as assistant principals. It will do no good to slim down the bureaucracy at the central office only to replace it with a new one in the school. Lead Teachers must create communities, not additional layers of bureaucracy to clog the system and frustrate their fellow teachers. Lead Teachers would derive their authority primarily from the respect of their professional colleagues. In such a relationship, teachers work together in a school, not separately in isolated classrooms; they take mutual responsibility for the curriculum and instruction on the basis of thinking together and individually about the substance of their work — children's learning — and how to make themselves better at it. They would also take collective responsibility for helping colleagues who were not performing up to par by arranging for coaching, technical assistance, coursework or other remediation that might be called for. In schools and districts in which Lead Teachers have assumed full responsibility for the school, they would be responsible for recommending

A small group of high schools scattered across the nation are beginning to change their approach to education in fundamental ways. Taking their lead from Theodore Sizer's Horace's Compromise, they have joined with Brown University to form the Coalition of Essential Schools. The Coalition grew out of The Study of High Schools, co-sponsored by the National Association of Secondary School Principals and the National Association of Independent Schools, which has set forth five "imperatives":

- Give room to teachers and students to work and learn in their own, appropriate ways

- Insist that students clearly exhibit mastery of their school work

- Get the incentives right for students and for teachers

- Focus the students' work on the use of their minds

- Keep the structure simple and flexible.

This prescription is now being adapted in different forms at 10 schools selected by the Coalition. Schools that choose to participate are encouraged to design their own curriculum based on the teachers' view of what's best for their students. No fixed form of school organization or instruction is required, just agreement with a common set of principles to guide the redesign effort. The principles incorporate the above imperatives along with such complementary ideas as: the governing practical metaphor of the school should be student-as-worker, rather than the more familiar teacher-as-deliverer-of-instructional-services.

At Westbury High in Houston the faculty is taking a fresh look at the instructional program absent the usual constraints imposed by the school district hierarchy. Teachers at Westbury were more than ready to try something radically different, even though their school was generally regarded among the best in the city. As Sharon Babson, an English teacher, put it: "All of us want this change. People who have not been in the classroom for 10 or 15 years are making decisions for us. They tell us what to teach and how to teach it and they don't even know the children. We know our students' needs. We can develop a curriculum as well as anyone else. I have no qualms about their defining the ends for the children. But they hired me to teach and they should trust me to do that."

Westbury's principal, Thomas C. Davis, is also enthusiastic, having come to the conclusion along with his teachers that however good the school looked from the outside it was falling way short of its potential. "It functions, but for the wrong reasons," he said. A new style of operating is emerging. "Basically, I'm taking myself out of a dictatorial kind of role," commented Davis, "and will move in the direction of He leads best who follows most."

In Manhattan's East Harlem a new school has been born, Central Park East. It, too, plans to follow the Coalition's principles, but will no doubt look different than Westbury. Starting with 90 seventh graders and five teachers, the school will add a new grade and five teachers each year until it becomes a full-fledged high school. Teachers will be able to spend much more time with each student because they will have 60 fewer students than is typical for such city schools. This is happening in spite of the fact that Central is getting no more money than any other New York public school. It is being done by limiting the school administrative staff to two people, a director and librarian, and having everyone engaged in teaching, including the director.

Based, in part, on Education Week, May 29, 1985

Each year for the last three years a cadre of seventh and eighth graders at Pyle Intermediate School in Montgomery County, Maryland, have spent one afternoon a week over a period of six weeks teaching science to children in the primary grades at a nearby elementary school. The Pyle students are volunteers who are trained by the primary teachers and their intermediate school teachers to use hands-on science learning experiments as a part of the regular instructional program in science at Burning Tree Elementary School. The program was conceived by two senior specialists in instruction and science education at the Maryland State Department of Education. The state agency originally provided funding for the six hours of training which the tutors receive before they begin their assignments. A mini-grant from the County now covers the costs.

There is a well-planned written curriculum which contains one lesson a week designed to be a hands-on inquiry experience. It is this lesson that the intermediate students are trained to teach. Each week, the same group of 42 young teachers come to Burning Tree for two hours and work with a group of four to six students each. The same adolescent teacher works with the same group of students every time, building continuity and a comfortable working relationship. To date, curricula have been developed in several areas including Light and Color, Electricity and Magnetism, and Outdoor Biology.

dismissal, subject to established procedures.

Professional practice partnerships organize themselves in a variety of ways, depending on the nature of their practice, the expertise of individual partners and the work style they find most congenial and efficient. Schools are similarly diverse in staff composition, size and clientele. Consequently, there is no hard and fast formulation of organizational structure that will prove most appropriate in all situations. Schools will divide responsibilities among Lead Teachers and others in different ways. Some Lead Teachers will take overall responsibility for the work of groups of professional teachers, while others serve as consultants or experts on particular areas of the curriculum. Roles will also change depending on the task. What is central is that, by vesting responsibility for instruction in Lead Teachers, schools will capitalize on the knowledge and skills of its most capable staff and create a career path worth pursuing.

Time. Fundamental to our conception of a workable professional environment that fosters learning is more time for all professional teachers to reflect, plan, and discuss teaching innovations and problems with their colleagues. Providing this additional time requires additional staff to support the professional teachers, technology that relieves teachers of much routine instructional and administrative work, a radical reorganization of work roles to make the most efficient use of staff in a collegial environment, and a new approach to the use of space.

Support Staff. Among the additional people needed to support the professional teacher are:

- A wide range of paid aides, technicians and assistants, providing clerical support and other administrative services, some of whom will be on career tracks leading to professional teacher status

- Interns and residents in the schools drawn from graduate teacher education programs, and instructors who have graduated from college but have not yet begun professional teacher education

- People with special skills or knowledge made available through partnerships with local business groups, community organizations, and colleges and universities

- High school and college students serving as coaches, tutors and aides

The use of high school and college students as teaching assistants is of special interest to the Task Force. The literature on students teaching students is very impressive. The student who is tutored is almost always helped; the student who tutors usually benefits even more. A great expansion in the numbers of students tutoring and coaching other students would promote significant gains in student achievement and permit teachers to spend more time working with small groups.

The Task Force has not attempted to devise a formal staffing structure into which various categories of support staff would fit. Professional teachers, within overall resource constraints set by the district, should make the decisions about the kinds of support they need and the necessary qualifications for that staff and take responsibility for the quality of their work.

The Use of Space. The traditional character of the teacher's classroom is so ingrained, the physical organization of schools so well established, that it is hard to grasp how school space might be differently used. Yet the collegial approach to school organization is unlikely to work, and additional staff are unlikely to contribute, unless some classes can be small and others large. Usage of space must be flexible so some students can work alone and others in small groups or with teachers, or a tutor.

Staffing Ratios. The Task Force emphasizes that support staff should be added to existing teacher staffing levels, not substituted for teachers. The ratio of students to professional teachers must remain stable.

School Leadership and the Role of the Principal. No organization can function well without strong and effective leadership and schools are no exception. But the single model for leadership found in most schools is better suited to business or government than to the function of education. The model of a non-teaching principal as head of the school can work in support of the collegial style of schooling we propose, but there are many other models that should be tried. Among them are schools headed by the Lead Teachers acting as a committee, one of whom acts like a managing partner in a professional partnership. In such schools, the teachers might hire the administrators, rather than the

other way around. Once the fundamental idea that the primary source of expertise for improving schools lies within them, many ways to organize for leadership are possible.

School-Site Budgeting and State Deregulation. It is essential to this plan that school staff be given freedom to determine how available resources will be used within constraints imposed by clearly stated goals and an effective accountability system. Principals now typically have very small discretionary funds. The services they need are generally located and controlled at the district level. In those circumstances, it is unreasonable to hold the principal and teachers responsible for the outcome.

It would be far more efficient to establish most school district instructional and other services as "cost centers" which have to sell their services to the schools in order to survive. Put another way, most of the budget for school district instructional services should be allocated to the school level, and the principal and teachers should together decide what services to buy and where.

This approach to decisionmaking would make it necessary for federal and state governments, school boards, and superintendents to greatly reduce the number of rules now on the books that constrain the kinds of decisions just described. That is an enormous job. It must be done with a great deal of sensitivity to the underlying rationale that created many of the rules in the first place. Some of those rules exist to make sure that the needs of at-risk populations are met. Those rules should not be relaxed, to say

The primary grade teachers value this individualized and small group experience for their students, which they could not provide by themselves. The primary grade students obviously adore working with the older students. There is regularly an oversupply of students signing up to be tutors. Curriculum specialists view it as a way to enhance science education at the primary level but see other values as well. It is an opportunity to support the interest these middle school children already have in science. And, it is clearly a way to involve these youngsters in thinking about becoming teachers. As young adolescents they bring some specific teaching skills to the job. Motivated to be effective teachers, they are flexible in working with the children and have good ideas about classroom management.

Growing out of a National Science Foundation project at the Smithsonian Institution, this activity, known as the Cross-Age Science Teaching Project, has now spread to inner-city schools in Baltimore where high school students and Towson State University students serve as tutors and to rural Dorchester County on Maryland's eastern shore.

A National Board for Professional Teaching Standards should be created to establish standards for high levels of competence in the teaching profession, to assess the qualifications of those seeking board certification, and to grant certificates to those who meet the standards.

1. The Board would grant Teacher's Certificates that attest to a high level of competence. It would also grant Advanced Teacher's Certificates that indicate outstanding teaching competence and demonstrated ability for school leadership.

2. In developing its standards, the Board should determine what teachers need to know and what they should be able to do.

3. The Board should work with institutions engaged in preparing prospective teachers to assist them in preparing candidates for certification.

4. A majority of the members of the National Board should be elected by Board-certified teachers.

5. Candidates for Board certification should be able to choose the means of preparation that best suits their needs.

6. The assessment of candidates for Board certification will require geographically decentralized administration. State or regional organizations of certified teachers should be created by the National Board to oversee Board functions at the regional and state level.

nothing of eliminated, until another set of rules, relating to the outcomes desired for those students, are in place and the means of assuring performance against the goals for those children are established through law or regulation.

Balancing Autonomy and Accountability. While it is important that teachers be invested with the authority and responsibility to exercise their professional judgment over a wide range of matters over which they currently have little control, that judgment, as we just noted, must be subject to certain constraints. Governing authorities will have to develop means to assure themselves that students are making satisfactory progress toward agreed upon goals. They will also have to be prepared to take action to either reduce teacher discretion or change the makeup of the school leadership team if student learning falls substantially below expectations. In effect, teachers have to be prepared to accept a greater degree of accountability in return for increased discretion. These matters are dealt with at greater length below.

Schools Where Professionals Teach. Schools should be exciting places for both teachers and students. With goals for student progress clear, professional teachers would be free to work with students to chart courses enabling each student to attain those goals. As the weight of the current bureaucratic environment is lifted and support staff take over many non-instructional tasks, professional teachers can concentrate on inspiring, coaching, guiding, and motivating students, and applying other resources, including

technology, to the task of improving student learning. Teachers can help each other analyze student problems, work with parents, help students master particularly tough concepts, develop materials and curricula, organize the work of the support staff, hire new staff and decide how to allocate the budget among competing claims. Such schools will provide a greatly improved environment for teaching.

New Standards for Excellence in Teaching

The last three years of education reform have produced a political axiom: those political leaders who are convinced of the importance of education are willing to risk their careers on proposals to improve teachers' pay and working conditions substantially — sometimes dramatically. However, they will not, or feel they cannot do so unless the public is persuaded that the teachers they spend more money on are fully capable of doing the job that now needs to be done.

This is hard for many teachers to accept, because they know that their earnings in real terms declined for a long time, while others' pay climbed. Their pay is also low to begin with compared to that of other college graduates. Increased pay, therefore, should not be contingent on meeting some new standard, they say. They take the position: we met the standards in place, and that have remained in place, for entering the teaching occupation and have met the standards for performance in the workplace. It is unfair to change those standards in midstream. And last, but hardly least, who is go-

State licensing authorities, which will continue to be responsible for licensing teachers to practice, should strengthen their standards and involve teachers in designing these new standards.

1. Board certification initially would be voluntary. In time, the Board's standards should be incorporated in the structure of state standards.

2. Anticipating the availability of Board-certified teachers, state officials should draft plans to offer districts incentives to hire such teachers in appropriate roles, and to provide for the equitable distribution of such teachers among districts of different tax capacity.

3. Licensure of participants in alternate route programs should meet a standard that is at least as high as that required of applicants from regular programs.

As post-graduate programs of teacher education are developed, the states and voluntary accreditation organizations should set and vigorously enforce high standards for such programs.

Appropriate state authorities should announce a date beyond which emergency licenses to teach will not be granted and licensed teachers will not be permitted to teach "out of subject."

ing to decide which teachers are qualified, on the basis of what criteria?

Both views are valid, as the Task Force sees it, and not irreconcilable. Dramatic improvements for teachers are not likely unless teachers clearly meet high standards of preparation and skill, but it is indeed unfair to those now in place to change the rules all at once. The proposals that follow are framed in this light.

As teaching makes the transition from occupation to profession, it can draw for inspiration on the experience of other professions. In no area is this more true than with respect to professional standards.

Virtually every occupation regarded by the public as a true profession has codified the knowledge, the specific expertise, required by its practitioners, and has required that those who wish to practice that profession with the sanction of its members demonstrate that they have a command of the needed knowledge and the ability to apply it. That is, the leading members of the profession decide what professionals in that area need to know and be able to do. They capture that knowledge in an assessment or examination and administer that examination to people who want a certificate saying they passed the assessment.

Certification is usually different from licensure. The profession issues the certificate. The state issues the license. The certificate means the profession itself pronounces the certificate holder fully competent to perform at a high professional standard. The license

indicates that the licensee meets the minimum standard established by the state to legally practice in the state. (We should note in passing that, in education, the terminology is unusual, in that what we are here describing as licensure is generally referred to as certification.) The state standard is designed to ensure the public safety; to signify that in the state's judgment the holder of a license will not endanger the safety of a client. In some professions, and some states, the basis for certification and licensure is identical. In others, the basis for certification and licensure is very different.

The issue of standards, however, is hardly limited to licensure and certification. What standards, for example, ought to be used to determine admission to professional education, graduation from professional education, and accreditation of professional education institutions?

One of the most important questions the Task Force had to deal with is the effect of the imposition of standards in these many arenas on the racial composition of the teaching force. Minority candidates have frequently experienced failure rates in the neighborhood of 70 percent or more when taking the examinations recently put in place by many states to qualify people for entrance into teaching. Will raising the standards even higher further reduce the flow of minority graduates into teaching? Is there a way to avoid that outcome?

These issues are addressed in this section of our report. We begin with the central issue of licensure and certification and then turn to the others.

A National Board for Professional Teaching Standards. The Task Force proposes creation of a National Board for Professional Teaching Standards. The Board's primary function would be to establish standards for high professional teaching competence and issue certificates to people who meet those standards.

The Board would issue two certificates: a Teacher's Certificate, and an Advanced Teacher's Certificate. The first would establish a high entry level standard for teachers. The second would be an advanced standard, signifying the highest levels of competence as a teacher and possession of the qualities needed for leadership in the schools. Certificates at both levels would be specific to subjects taught and grade ranges and could be endorsed on examination for other areas of specialization. In time, the Board would establish standards for recertification comparable to those that exist in other professions.

A majority of the membership of the Board would be chosen by holders of the certificates to be issued by the Board. Certificate holders could participate in the election process in a variety of ways, including election of state or regional representatives, who would in turn elect Board members. The balance of the Board would be made up of other education professionals, public officials, and public members. Governors, chief state school officers, and school administrators, for example, would be represented on the Board.

The Board is not likely to succeed unless the standards it sets are high, represent a broad consensus of those concerned with public education, and, above all, represent the views of the developing profession itself on the question of what standard of practice can be considered fully professional.

The Board would also have other responsibilities: to develop a code of ethics for the profession; discipline people violating the code; and maintain a register of Teachers and Advanced Teachers. Other tasks might include making recommendations on standards for hiring teachers and school support staff and sponsoring research on the labor market for teachers and the status of teachers and teaching.

The assessment itself should enable the Board to judge the quality of candidates' general education, their mastery of the subjects they will teach, their knowledge of good teaching practices in general and their mastery of the techniques required to teach specific subjects. The assessment should determine whether candidates have the capacity to reach, motivate and support the learning of students from many different backgrounds.

To accomplish these objectives, the assessment techniques used will have to go far beyond multiple choice examinations. They will have to employ state-of-the-art techniques of formal examination as well as rely in part on the observations of highly trained and experienced teachers of candidates' actual teaching.

In determining both what is worth knowing about teaching and what a teacher should be able to do, the Board will have to rely on the growing body of research on teaching and learning in addition to the experience of outstanding teachers. The Task Force is particularly concerned that the assessment take into account the accumulated wisdom of teachers. This is true in general, but nowhere more so than with respect to teachers who have been particularly successful in promoting the learning of children from minority and low-income backgrounds.

With respect to equity issues, the orientation of the Board toward its assessment and certification role is crucial. The object is to design a process that helps as many as possible reach a high standard. The Board should not just devise assessment materials and methods, but also work with institutions engaged in preparing prospective teachers by providing materials and information that will help candidates understand the demands of the assessment process and judge their readiness to be examined. Particular attention should be paid to institutions enrolling large numbers of minority candidates, so that these institutions can do the best possible job of preparing their students for the assessment. The problem of underrepresentation of minorities in the teaching force is deeply rooted and especially troubling and will not be solved by the actions of the National Board alone, however farsighted. But there is much the Board can do to help.

The Task Force believes the assessment should be in three stages. The first, related to subject matter, would typically be taken on graduation from college. The second, testing student mastery of the material usually covered in professional educational coursework, whenever the candidate was ready. The third, based on observation of the candidate's actual teaching over a substantial period, would be the last stage. Each of these stages should be designed not to eliminate candidates but to identify deficiencies in preparation that need to be corrected before a certificate is granted. Each candidate should have as much time as is needed to complete the assessment process.

The administration of the assessment will clearly have to be decentralized to guarantee easy access for candidates. The National Board would create state or regional affiliates composed of Board-certified teachers to oversee the assessment process and perform other functions on behalf of the Board.

The certification process is envisioned by the Task Force as completely voluntary. There would be no requirement imposed on new teachers or teachers currently in the workforce to participate. But the Task Force expects that many teachers will wish to do so, because the certificate will be an unambiguous statement that its holder is a highly qualified teacher. Certificate holders can expect to be eagerly sought by states and districts that pride themselves on the quality of their schools. Compensation systems should reflect the value of Board certification. In time, many states are likely to incorporate the national certification standard into their licensing standards. Some might choose to waive their licensing requirements for people holding a Board certificate. Others might make Board certification a prerequisite for licensing, adding their own requirements to the national standard as they think appropriate.

States that waive their licensure requirements for those who have "passed their boards" will be able thereby to create an alternate route into the profession that will enlarge the pool of able people who can be attracted to the profession. In the period before Board-certified teachers are available in large numbers, those states with alternative route programs should make sure that licenses are granted only to teachers that meet performance standards at least as high as those designed for the graduates of regular teacher education programs.

Standards for Teacher Education. In most states, a license to practice as a teacher is granted to students who graduate from institutions with teacher preparation programs approved by the state. This is known as the "program approval" process. Beyond the admissions criteria normally employed by the institution, there is generally no special regulation of admission to teacher education institutions by the state.

Long before the Board produces its first assessment, its standards will begin to be available as a resource to those shaping teacher education programs, and setting standards for graduation. Institutions and those responsible for state program approval should take advantage of Board standards to raise the quality of teacher education.

The other primary agent of quality in

teacher education programs is accreditation through voluntary association of the institutions themselves. Although current excess capacity in many teacher education institutions creates strong pressure to keep accreditation standards low, higher accreditation standards are now in place. The Task Force believes accreditation can prove a powerful force for improvement, as it has been in other professions, if schools of education voluntarily set and enforce high standards. This will be especially important as new graduate teacher education programs are developed.

Enforcing Current Standards. As demand rises faster than supply, many states and districts are ignoring the standards already in place as they seek to staff their classrooms. When standards are ignored in order to fill vacancies, the public is misled into believing that things are getting better when in fact they might be getting worse. This is the case when students are made to take more demanding academic courses and there are not enough teachers qualified to teach them.

State officials should declare a date beyond which the state will not permit districts to employ unqualified teachers, that is, hire teachers who do not meet existing licensure requirements, or permit districts to assign teachers to teach subjects they are not qualified to teach. Such action will reveal the true extent of the teacher shortage and generate pressure to pay teachers at competitive market rates.

Preparing for National Certification. Although it will be a few years before the National Board grants its first certificate, there are a number of constructive steps that state bodies responsible for licensure can take. First, would be to bolster their current standards. This will be made easier as the National Board issues preliminary standards that will later be used in the assessment. The design of new and improved state standards should be accomplished with the full involvement of the state's teachers. Second, in anticipation of Board-certified teachers being available for hire, state authorities should begin drafting plans to offer districts incentives to engage such teachers in appropriate roles and at higher rates of pay than teachers without Board certification.

The availability of Board-certified teachers is likely to lead to intense competition among districts for their services, since, for the first time, local boards and parents will be able to identify reliably teachers who have met a high standard. Districts of modest and low tax capacity may be at a special disadvantage in this competition, aggravated by the fact that these teachers will come on the market during a period of severe teacher shortage. States, therefore, need to take a variety of steps to provide for the equitable distribution of Board-certified teachers. (Possible steps are discussed further in the section on Teacher Salaries and Benefits.)

The benefits of establishing the National Board are many. Once the Board is in place, the profession will find itself, for the first time, in control of the definition of what it means to be a professional teacher. As the high standard set by the Board becomes widely known, public confidence in teachers will

rise. Teachers, having set that standard, will have a considerable investment in maintaining and enforcing it. The certificates granted by the Board will lead to more career mobility and greater opportunities for advancement in the profession. The states will find that they can take advantage of the investment required to create a rigorous assessment of teacher competence, without having to bear the full costs of its development. Nor will they have to do battle with the profession over standards. Accrediting organizations will have a standard for their work accepted by the whole profession. School boards and others will be able to hire and promote against a clear standard of professional competence.

Restructuring Teacher Education

Teacher education must meet much higher standards. The focus must be on what teachers need to know and be able to do. Raising standards for entry into the profession is likely to give the public confidence that the teachers they hire will be worth the increased salary and worthy of the increased autonomy we advocate. These policies will most certainly fail, however, if the education of teachers is not greatly improved. Otherwise, new teachers may be unable to perform up to the new expectations.

The initial preparation of teachers is typically carried out entirely at the undergraduate level, though some states require an additional year of study, usually within a fixed period following initial certification. Generally, graduate schools of

States should abolish the undergraduate degree in education and make professional teacher education a graduate level enterprise, building on a base of sound undergraduate education in the arts and sciences.

1. Master in Teaching degree programs should be developed. They should emphasize systematic study of teaching and clinical experience, including internships and residencies in the schools.

2. Admission should be contingent on applicants' mastery of the basic skills and knowledge expected of all college graduates.

3. The graduate schools of education should design these new programs to make it possible for students to make up during their graduate education substantive course work missed in college. The time allowed to obtain a graduate degree should take this requirement into account.

4. Special financial incentives should be offered by the state and others to students of exceptional academic ability and to minority group members who qualify to attend graduate teacher education institutions.

education prepare educational administrators and specialists, not classroom teachers. Subject matter preparation, however, is not the responsibility of departments or colleges of education, but rather of the arts and sciences departments of the parent institution. Prospective elementary teachers take a substantial number of courses in education, secondary teachers only a few. The result is that elementary teachers have relatively little exposure to the subjects they will teach and secondary teachers very little preparation for the act of teaching the subjects in which they have majored.

Substantial numbers of college graduates failed recently instituted examinations that are mainly tests of reading comprehension. Many, of course, have completed college level work. But too few completed academically demanding undergraduate programs of a level of difficulty comparable to that, say, typically completed by students expecting to become doctors, architects or engineers.

Some teacher education programs demand rigorous preparation of their students, but too many produce graduates who complain that their education courses failed to prepare them for teaching. They lacked knowledge in essential functions such as maintaining discipline, guiding students over predictably difficult topics, inspiring student effort, and recognizing and responding to problems of students from varied social, economic and racial backgrounds. Many of the same graduates also voice similar criticisms about their courses in the arts and sciences.

Teachers need a command of the subjects they teach, a sound grasp of the techniques of teaching those subjects, information about research on teaching, and an understanding of children's growth and development and of their different needs and learning styles.

Examinations can play an important part in improving the professional competence of teachers, but they are not alone sufficient to advance the practice of teaching. A balanced strategy for the improvement of teaching would entail equal emphasis on standards and on the improvement of education for teachers. A significant investment in research, curriculum, and clinical practice will be required.

While the proposed National Board for Professional Teaching Standards must base its assessment on a determination of what teachers need to know and what they should be able to do, it will not attempt to define a national curriculum for teacher education. Graduate programs should develop out of a systematic understanding of practice rather than uniform national standards alone. The locus of responsibility for this understanding rests with professional university programs constructed by university faculties in collaboration with school professionals. No occupation has ever successfully become a profession without a strong association with higher education.

New policies are needed for teacher education that recognize its pivotal role in strengthening the teaching profession. Sweeping changes are required both in the institutional structure of teacher education and in

"Our universities must respond to the crisis in public education. As the educators of most teachers and administrators in public schools, we have some responsibility for conditions in them. We have outlined a program of action aimed at dramatically improving the quality of America's teachers and at improving the teaching profession. We have committed ourselves to work for these improvements—in our universities. Without the sorts of change outlined here, the quality of teaching and learning in the public schools cannot improve.

". . . our proposal is hardly radical. For American universities know quite well how to provide outstanding professional education. The best professional education in medicine, public affairs, business and law, that can be found in the world is found here in the United States. There is no doubt that our universities can do an equally outstanding job for teachers. The only question is whether they will."

Tomorrow's Teachers: A Report of the Holmes Group, *1986*

To assure that teachers, along with all other students, receive adequate preparation in their field of study, college faculties and disciplinary societies should undertake a thorough reexamination of undergraduate programs in the arts and sciences to ensure their appropriateness for the preparation of professional teachers.

The following steps should be taken to assure that professional teachers are properly trained to implement new programs at the local level, remain current in their fields, and have an opportunity to prepare for the Board assessment leading to the advanced teaching certificate:

1. State and local policy should stimulate colleges, universities and a variety of other providers to develop programs of continuing education to keep teachers abreast of the field, and to prepare Board-certified teachers for the Advanced Teaching Certificate:

2. Districts and teachers should work together to establish staff development centers run by very able teachers to meet local continuing education and training needs.

3. In time, Board standards for recertifying teachers should be used as a guide for continuing education.

The states, the federal government and business should provide financial aid for the graduate education of highly qualified applicants interested in teaching in fields experiencing severe shortages.

the curriculum offered to the students. Though much has been learned in recent years that can inform the education of teachers, an even greater effort must now be made to provide a solid foundation of research under an intellectual framework that teacher educators can use to develop the kinds of teachers the nation needs.

New policies for teacher education must meet other criteria. The first requirement is that they produce teachers with the necessary knowledge and skills. The second, that they prepare people who perform the kinds of roles described in this report with a high degree of competence. The third, that they enable teaching to draw on the largest possible pool of qualified people and not exclude people who did not take education courses as undergraduates. Fourth, the expense of teacher education must be reasonably related to the lifetime salaries teachers can expect to make. Finally, teacher education should result in candidates who are well prepared for National Board assessments.

Undergraduate Education. Four years of college education is not enough time to master the subjects to be taught and acquire the skills to teach them. The undergraduate years should be wholly devoted to a broad liberal education and a thorough grounding in the subjects to be taught. The professional education of teachers should therefore take place at the graduate level. An alternative might be to combine the undergraduate program and a graduate degree program, awarding both the bachelor's and the graduate degree. In either case, the states and higher education institutions should abolish the bachelor's degree in education.

Relegating the professional education of teachers to the graduate level does not, however, mean that the states or colleges and universities can be indifferent to the quality or kind of undergraduate education received by prospective teachers.

The fact that some people who are unable to spell, write, speak grammatically, or solve arithmetical word problems now graduate from college and become teachers is an indictment of the institutions of higher education and licensing authorities.

College graduates going on to professional graduate education should have a rigorous undergraduate curriculum that embraces a common core of history, government, science, literature and the arts. That core should develop the essential skills of comprehension, computation, writing, speaking, and clear thinking. It should deepen appreciation of our history and culture, foster an understanding of the theory and application of science and technology, develop aesthetic sensibilities, and inspire creative impulses.

Elementary teachers need such solid undergraduate preparation as much as secondary teachers. Elementary and secondary teachers impart our common culture, heritage and values to our children. It is terribly important that they be fully prepared for this task. Elementary teachers are typically responsible for a much wider range of subjects than secondary school teachers, but this cannot excuse a less than rigorous grasp of the material for which they are responsible. Elementary teachers must be able to demonstrate a substantive understanding of each subject they teach. This may mean that

Stanford University has been operating a multi-disciplinary program in human biology for 16 years that in many ways suggests a new model of undergraduate education. The program has a director, a set of student advisers and is staffed by faculty from across the university. Professors come from the departments of law, psychiatry, anthropology, geology, genetics, radiology, chemistry, sociology and biological sciences to name a few. What distinguishes it from other interdisciplinary programs around the country is a special effort to discourage dabbling. The program emphasizes instead in-depth study of a particular field, the application of knowledge to practical problems and the opportunity to contribute to on-going work in the field through internships.

Coursework begins by exposing students to central ideas in the natural and social sciences, presented in a manner that allows them to see the broad picture of how the various fields intersect with one another. This perspective then provides a backdrop for more specialized study of particular subjects.

Students are expected to do advanced coursework in an area where they have a special interest and meet a set of core criteria that have been established for the program. In addition to establishing a basic understanding of the natural, social and behavioral sciences, grounding in statistics and the fundamentals of public policy are part of the curriculum. Students are encouraged to undertake honors research as an extension of their area of concentration.

These requirements spring from the program designers' belief that society today, and in the decades to come, faces a range of complex problems that will not be amenable to quick technological fixes or simple political or economic remedies. H. Craig Heller, the program's chairman, says: "Scientific approaches to these problems are essential, but deeper understanding and formulation of appropriate policies require concomitant appreciation of influences which drive human behavior: economic factors, social structures, political systems, and cultural practices and beliefs."

While the program has a set of rigorous core requirements, it remains flexible in order that students may follow their intellectual interests and instincts in whatever direction seems most appropriate. In consultation with a faculty advisor, the student aides, juniors and seniors in the program, help their fellow classmates custom design advanced coursework and internships best suited to each person's strengths and inclinations.

The University Teaching Center at Carnegie-Mellon University was established to improve the instructional skills of teaching faculty in undergraduate and graduate courses.

The concept of a university teaching center is not unique to Carnegie-Mellon. What is unusual is the attempt to encourage the valuing of good teaching and the resulting bottom-up approach to staff development. President Richard Cyert initiated the idea by having Edwin Fenton seek advice from the university community about what a center ought to do and the kind of assistance they would value. Students were also surveyed to ascertain their special perspective on what constituted good teaching practice. What evolved has become a vehicle for building a "culture of teaching" at this research university.

The Center's objective is to build the capacity for staff development into individual departments on campus. The Center, therefore, has only one regular staff person and uses faculty members on a rotating basis to teach workshops and seminars. Prof. Fenton, a historian and faculty member of long standing, became the Director. He offers a short course in teaching for six weeks on a continuing basis throughout the academic year. The course includes the identification of teaching improvement practices, how to develop a good syllabus, teaching techniques for discussion and lecture, and techniques for self-evaluation.

In addition to the course, the UTC has video taped about one-third of the Carnegie Mellon faculty and organized workshops in teaching for teaching assistants led by some 40 faculty members. A handbook, About Teaching at Carnegie Mellon, *published in 1984, draws on research about effective university teaching and on consultations with students, administrators and faculty at the university.*

Participation is open to all faculty members who also may receive individual assistance as well as enroll in structured programs. UTC director Fenton stresses that the center is directed at the improvement of teaching and is completely separate from the faculty evaluation process.

elementary teachers will have to organize themselves differently and teach fewer subjects.

Many students' failure to perform close to their potential starts in upper elementary school, where the material is often so boring or poorly presented that student interest or self confidence wanes. We know that other countries demand significantly more from their elementary students and that effective American teachers help average sixth grade students learn to write well and master mathematical concepts that are not typically taught until high school. Such teachers know their subject and can make it come alive. All our teachers need to have this capacity.

Colleges and universities have long complained about the poor performance of the schools, and many have acted as if their duty to improve pre-college education had been discharged by raising their admission standards. Colleges and universities have failed to provide the education that school teachers need. Higher education leaders must seize the initiative and play their part in strengthening the schools.

Arts and sciences faculties must join their education colleagues, and, together with the leaders of professional and disciplinary societies, begin by undertaking a thorough review of the undergraduate curriculum for the education of prospective teachers. This does not constitute a call for a ''watered down'' curriculum but a strengthened one. Such a strengthened curriculum would not, of course, preclude provision for students with an early interest in teaching, who should

be able to gain some exposure to the underlying theory, research, and history of education during their undergraduate years. This might involve taking related coursework in psychology or sociology or taking courses offered by the school of education. The schools of education along with the National Board might also issue recommendations for undergraduates who think they might be interested in going on to post-graduate work in education.

Arts and sciences faculty also need to give careful scrutiny to their undergraduate majors. These majors are typically constructed with the needs of other professions in mind. There is no reason why, for example, the undergraduate major in physics should pay more attention to the needs of prospective professional physics researchers than those of future physics teachers. As we have noted, by 1992, more than 200,000 college graduates a year are required for teaching. This represents a challenge and responsibility for college and university officers and faculty of such magnitude and urgency that it deserves their immediate attention.

University presidents should set a high priority for development of strong undergraduate programs for all students, the development of post-graduate professional education for teaching, and close cooperation between the faculties responsible for education and the arts and sciences.

The Master in Teaching Degree Program. A newly developed Master in Teaching degree should set a new standard for the professional preparation of teachers. It would

Kenyon College of Ohio, concerned about the shortage of academically strong students entering the teaching force, has, in conjunction with Bank Street College of Education and Columbia University's Teachers College, developed a new program to attract students to a career in teaching. Known as 5-STEP (Student Teacher Education Program), it brings Kenyon students to New York after their junior year to study for two semesters and one summer session. They attend Bank Street for preparation in early childhood, elementary or museum education, or Teachers College for secondary education. After their year in New York, students return to Kenyon to complete a fifth year of study and receive both a BA and a Masters degree. Very capable students who might otherwise never have considered teaching as an option now have a new route into the work force.

The program was initiated with the help of the U.S. Department of Education's Fund for the Improvement of Postsecondary Education which was interested in encouraging the emergence of new avenues to engage graduates of liberal arts colleges in teaching. In the coming year, other members of the Great Lakes Colleges Association may make this alternative path into teaching available to their students.

"Teaching is a solo act and most of the time you don't know whether you're doing it well or very badly." Countering this truism is at the heart of the Schenley High School Teacher Center, according to Mary Finley, a Pittsburgh biology teacher with 18 years of experience.

The high school faculty of the Pittsburgh Public Schools has on the average 16 years of experience in the school district, most of those years in a single school. Typical of high school teachers, they have little exposure to recent developments in instructional techniques, and the demands of teaching limit the opportunities to renew and refresh their knowledge of their content fields. The promise of doing both provided the rationale for creating the Schenley Center and led to early support from Ford Foundation.

The Center was conceived as part of a plan designed to foster both improved student achievement and staff performance and to counter the high dropout rates which trouble Pittsburgh as they do other urban school districts. In this case, teacher renewal was seen as part of the solution. The center is part of an operating comprehensive high school. The school's residential teaching staff teaches a reduced class load and works with the visiting teachers who come from high schools all over the district.

prepare candidates to become competent teachers and pass the assessment procedures required for Board certification; it would serve as a foundation on which a career in teaching and further studies could be built.

The purposes of the graduate program would be to prepare candidates to take maximum advantage of the research on teaching and the accumulated knowledge of exceptional teachers. It would develop their instructional and management skills, cultivate the habit of reflecting on their own practice of teaching, and lay a strong base for continuing professional development.

One possible model for developing these skills involves a two-year program of studies. The first year begins with a summer session in which the student takes a full load of courses designed to provide basic instruction in teaching. During the following nine months, the candidate serves as an intern in a school that has a diverse student population and concurrently takes several graduate courses. The following summer, the candidate again carries a full load of graduate courses designed to build on the student's initial teaching experience.

The second year of the program would consist of residency in a school, with the candidate assuming substantial teaching responsibilities under the supervision of Lead Teachers. These teachers should also hold appointments in the graduate school in which the candidate is enrolled. Additional graduate coursework may be required during this residency year.

Many variations of this approach are possible. In any event, education school faculties will themselves decide, as they should, what form graduate study should take. What is essential is a strong element of field-based preparation, emphasizing opportunities for careful reflection on teaching integrated with a demanding program of academic coursework.

"Clinical" schools, selected from among public schools and staffed for the preparation of teachers, must be developed to make this successful. These institutions, having an analogous role to teaching hospitals, should be outstanding public schools working closely with schools of education. The Lead Teachers in these schools should hold adjunct appointments in the school of education and serve as core instructional staff in the Master in Teaching degree program. The clinical schools should exemplify the collegial, performance-oriented environment that newly certified teachers should be prepared to establish. By connecting elementary and secondary education and higher education in a much more direct way than is typically the case now, these new institutions will create a valuable linkage between the elementary and secondary schools, the schools of education and the arts and sciences departments.

The second approach to instruction that should be incorporated into the design of the post-graduate programs is the case method, well developed in law and business, but almost unknown in teaching instruction. Teaching "cases" illustrating a great variety of teaching problems should be developed as a major focus of instruction.

Adoption of the Master in Teaching degree program raises important considerations regarding time and cost, interim procedures for certification and licensing and incentives for students to pursue the degree.

Candidates must have as much time to complete the program as they need to prepare for certification, to address gaps in their undergraduate preparation, and to ease the transition for mid-career professionals who consider entering teaching. However, admission to the Master in Teaching degree program should be contingent on applicants' mastery of the basic skills and knowledge expected of all college graduates.

Though Master in Teaching degree program candidates will be paid during internship and residency, the costs to them of their graduate studies will be substantial. Financial assistance should be provided for highly talented students interested in graduate study to prepare themselves for fields in which substantial long term shortages exist. In the following section, there is a separate recommendation concerning fellowships for minority students. Here, we are concerned with such areas as mathematics and science, which are likely to be in short supply for many years to come, and are therefore likely to require special financial aid even after the main features of the Task Force plan are in place. The seriousness of the mathematics and science teacher shortage has motivated many people to believe that nothing less than a major program to meet this need will be required.

Finally, student interest in the Master in

Teaching degree in the short run will be limited if a license based on an undergraduate program confers the same advantages as the Master in Teaching. However, tying licensure to a single mode of preparation is not the policy the Task Force would recommend. Schools of education will continue to play the primary role in preparing the nation's teachers. Other providers may turn out to be important sources of professional education during the next decade as demand explodes. Their ability to serve this function should not be compromised by state licensing standards that are unduly restrictive. States can develop alternative routes to teacher preparation which meet standards equal to those in regular university programs. Board certification or an equivalent performance standard should be the measure of a candidate's readiness to teach, however he or she is prepared.

Continuing Education. The Task Force sees no reason to perpetuate a system of continuing education that determines teacher compensation on the basis of credits earned after becoming a teacher. Compensation should be based on proven competence, not time in the chair.

The need for relevant continuing education nevertheless remains strong. Teachers need staff development opportunities in order to design and implement local programs and to keep up with their fields. They need advanced education in order to reach the highest levels of their profession. Many who are now teaching will need opportunities for continuing education to help them prepare for their Board examinations.

They plan programs, teach seminars, run clinics on effective teaching, observe visiting teachers teach and are themselves observed. By the end of the 1986-7 school year nearly all of Pittsburgh's high school teachers will have spent an eight-week "mini-sabbatical" at Schenley. They will have participated in a program which focuses on instructional skills, content area update, adolescent development, and their individual interests which range from doing an internship with a local business to learning about applications of computer technology. While at the center, their classes are taught by replacement teachers who have gone through the Schenley program and are tenured, full-time teachers in the Pittsburgh schools.

After spending eight weeks at the Center as learners and part of a collegial teaching environment, the teachers return to their home schools. There they are expected to continue using the techniques they have learned. Their principals and department chairs have themselves been trained in clinical supervision and so changed expectations are shared. Superintendent Richard Wallace hopes that as a result of Schenley, every high school will, in effect, become a teacher learning center.

Based, in part, on the Ford Foundation Letter, *October 1, 1985*

This year, students at the University of California, Berkeley are working at Far West High School in Oakland as teaching assistants in Spanish, French, math and science classes and coaching the debate team. They are there as part of the University's work-study program which has been providing the Oakland schools with tutors for a number of years.

The University also has work-study contracts with the Berkeley and Richmond school districts that help needy college students pay for their education while tutoring minority and other children. This program pays college students from $7.50 to $9.00 per hour.

Riverside Unified School District in southern California employs tutors from Riverside City College, California State University at San Bernardino and the University of California, Riverside. Recently, the Gifted Education Program in Riverside engaged a California State University student to work in one of their elementary schools. She spent 10 to 15 hours per week in the classroom and earned $4.05 per hour. Eighty percent of her earnings came from federal student aid through the California State University Work-Study program. The school district paid the remaining 20 percent, plus an additional 10 percent for administrative costs.

In the University of California system alone, over 9,000 students participate in work-study programs. Most jobs are on-campus, but many are in schools working with disadvantaged youngsters.

School or district-wide staff development centers are one of the most effective means of helping teachers design and implement local programs.

The eventual adoption of a periodic recertification requirement by the Board will provide a strong incentive for teachers to stay current. The Board should be organized in close association with the current subject-oriented teachers' associations such as the National Science Teachers Association. Such a structure would permit professionals themselves to decide what is important to keep up in the field, communicate it to the profession, and validate courses meeting their standards just as other professions control continuous upgrading of professional skills.

Finally, continuing education must play a central role in meeting the needs of teachers seeking the Advanced Certificate. These candidates must be acquainted with work at the frontiers of the subjects they teach. They need to be very familiar with a wide range of sophisticated materials, emerging uses of technology, and approaches available to help students with especially difficult problems. They need, too, to be knowledgeable about issues of educational policy, the philosophy of education, and technical aspects of measuring progress.

Because many Lead Teachers will play a central role in school decisionmaking, they should be prepared to organize the work of others, provide for staff development, help teachers to use technology effectively, participate in the allocation of resources and relate effectively to parents, the community at large and the school district administrative staff.

The Board's standards for the Advanced Teaching Certificate will serve as a guide for the continuing education of teachers who want to obtain that certificate. Graduate schools of education will need to create programs addressing the needs of the advanced assessment candidate. Although these need not be degree programs, universities may wish to create advanced degree programs for this purpose.

State and local policy can serve to stimulate colleges, universities and a variety of other providers to meet this continuing education challenge by creating a host of incentives. Recognizing the Advanced Certificate in compensation plans is the one act that would probably provide the greatest leverage.

The Training of Support Staff. A considerable expansion of the support staff, including people who are themselves students, requires extensive staff training and development. Research on students tutoring other students shows the best results when the tutors receive some formal training for the task, even if only for a few days. The same should be true of others serving in non-professional support roles.

Districts should plan carefully for training all those who serve for more than a few days in auxiliary roles. The most qualified teachers in the district should decide what training is needed and how it should be provided: by colleges or universities, by the district itself, or by an outside vendor.

Minority Teachers

The public schools educate and socialize the nation's children. Schools form children's opinions about the larger society and their own futures. The race and background of their teachers tells them something about authority and power in contemporary America. These messages influence children's attitudes toward school, their academic accomplishments, and their views of their own and others' intrinsic worth. The views they form in school about justice and fairness also influence their future citizenship.

The key to quality instruction for disadvantaged students, as for all students, is the capable teacher. However, these children, who have the strongest claim on the schools' resources to give them a fair start in life, have the least power to make good on that claim. For this reason, the Task Force has called the reader's attention to issues of equity in each section of these recommendations.

Those who call for higher standards for entrance into teaching have a special responsibility to prevent new barriers from reducing the proportion of minority teachers. The issue is how to produce enough minority candidates who can meet the high standards of the Board. Many prospective teachers from minority groups fail to meet high standards not for lack of ability but because the schools have failed to provide and demand what was needed for success.

The broad outlines of the problem can be seen in the numbers. First, Blacks, Hispanics and Asians account for a rising proportion of the school population. California now has a majority of minorities in the first three grades of its elementary schools, and 23 out of the 25 largest city school systems enroll a majority of minority students. By around the year 2000, one out of three Americans will be a member of a racial minority.

At the same time, children are getting poorer. Almost half the poor in the United States are children, and poor children tend to have a variety of medical and nutritional problems including unusually low birthweights, a factor associated with major learning difficulties. Ninety percent of the increase in children in poverty is accounted for by children born to single Black and Hispanic women. At the same time, projections of current trends indicate that Blacks will be only five percent of the teaching force by 1990. The prospects for other minorities being well represented in the teaching force also do not look promising. The college completion rates for most minority groups are very low. Only about seven percent of Hispanics, for example, complete college.

Attracting an increasing, rather than a decreasing, number of Blacks, Hispanics and Native Americans into teaching is partly a matter of recruitment. At the heart of the issue is the need to greatly increase the flow through the educational pipeline of members of these minority groups so they can join the pool of eligible candidates.

Minorities constitute close to 25 percent of the elementary and secondary student population. Just seeking a rough equivalence among new teachers, schools of education

A partnership of government, the private sector, the minority community, and the schools should be created to ensure an increasing number of minority teachers.

1. The commitments made since 1965 by the federal and state governments to meeting the needs of minority and low-income students should be reaffirmed and strengthened.

2. Partnerships involving business, higher education, community based organizations and schools that have been shown to be effective in providing support for minority children to meet high academic objectives should be widely emulated, with support from the states, business and private foundations.

3. States, corporations, colleges, community organizations and others should work together to put in place a comprehensive program for pre-college education of minority youth. A wide range of educational interventions should span the educational pipeline and include school and out-of-school programs such as tutoring, community service, counseling, summer and Saturday experiences and bridge programs between high school and college.

4. Federal and state governments, college officials, private philanthropies and others should strengthen and extend the reach of programs proven to be effective in recruiting minority students to college and retaining them. This should include:

   • Assisting the predominantly Black institutions of higher education prepare students for graduate professional education in teaching, and

   • Developing policies and programs that will increase the rate at which minorities, particularly Blacks and Hispanics, enter four-year colleges and universities and transfer from two-year community colleges to four-year colleges.

5. The federal government should establish a program to provide fellowships to minority students who enroll in professional teacher education programs at the graduate level. In return, recipients would commit themselves to a fixed period of teaching service.

Combined SAT Scores for College-Bound High School Seniors by Intended Field of Study

At both ability levels and for each ethnic group, the education major appears, on average, to draw the least able students.

Major	Blacks percentile			Mexican Americans percentile			Puerto Ricans percentile			Whites percentile		
	%	25	75	%	25	75	%	25	75	%	25	75
Arts & Humanities	8	556	810	10	622	913	9	594	892	10	763	1068
Biological Science	2	633	929	3	698	992	3	715	1023	3	863	1162
Health & Medicine	17	579	833	16	651	933	17	588	904	15	774	1073
Business	21	551	785	18	612	873	20	578	823	19	736	1012
Computer Science	16	571	813	11	641	927	14	583	890	9	795	1093
Engineering	11	648	954	13	730	1021	9	707	1047	12	885	1180
Social Sciences	15	562	818	9	651	943	8	627	916	18	762	1060
Education	3	511	722	5	587	835	4	543	819	5	702	973
Mean	715			796			766			932		

Source: Educational Testing Service, unpublished tabulations.

Mathematics, Engineering and Science Achievement (MESA) is designed to increase the numbers of underrepresented ethnic groups in these fields by providing precollege programs at both the high school and junior high school levels as well as a university retention program. Begun in 1970 with 25 students at the Oakland Technical School in California, MESA/California now involves over 4,000 students from 139 high schools. Related programs have begun in New Mexico, Colorado, Washington, Arizona and New York.

Selection for participation in the California program requires completion of Algebra I and enrollment in an academic math course. The students must have at least two years remaining before high school graduation. Students are selected for MESA/New Mexico at the 8th and 9th grade levels on the basis of an expressed interest in mathematics and science-related careers and are required to enroll in college preparatory mathematics and science courses.

The New Mexico program began in 1982 in cooperation with the University of New Mexico and the New Mexico Institute of Mining and Technology. It includes tutoring by engineers, scientists and college students and academic, university and career counseling. There are also field trips, scholarship incentive awards for students who maintain a high grade point average in advanced level college

preparatory mathematics, science and English courses, and summer enrichment and employment programs.

The results are impressive in California where the program has its longest track record. More than 90 percent of MESA high school graduates go on to college. MESA students achieve mathematics and verbal SAT scores that on average exceed those of non-MESA college-bound students by 75 and 35 points respectively. Among minority women high school graduates who participate, five times as many plan to become engineers as their non-MESA counterparts.

Based on Promoting Success Through Collaborative Ventures in Precollege Science and Mathematics, *National Association of Precollege Directors, 1985*

The Saturday Science Academy, part of the Atlanta University Resource Center for Science and Engineering, is devoted to increasing the number of minority and low-income students pursuing science and technical careers. The program engages students from grades 3-8 on 10 Saturday mornings to increase their awareness and skill levels in science, mathematics and communications.

Enrollment is free and instruction is provided by college faculty and other specialists in the field, along with high school teachers and graduate student assistants. Classes are 50 minutes each with no more than 5 minutes taken up with lecturing. The students actually "do science:" hands-on experience characterizes the science classes and the inquiry approach is used for teaching mathematics. Attention is given to helping students learn to express themselves clearly and creatively as the program seeks to improve their proficiency in writing and speaking. This is often accomplished through creative arts and drama.

The Center also sponsors the Summer Science, Engineering and Mathematics Institute and the Summer Enrichment Program. The former is an 8-week academic program for 60 juniors and seniors designed to strengthen their capabilities for academic work leading to careers in scientific and technical fields. All of the 289 students who completed the program between 1979 and 1982 have enrolled in college: 39 percent in engineering, 36 percent in the physical and biological sciences, 19 percent in mathematics and computer science and 6 percent in other subjects.

The Summer Enrichment Program in the sciences offers 30 college juniors and seniors from participating institutions in-depth and interdisciplinary studies that are not available on their own campuses.

would have to produce 50,000 minority Master in Teaching degree holders each year when hiring rates reach 200,000 teachers per year. Only 100,000 B.A. degrees were awarded to all minority students in the last year for which data are available. And, in recent years, the percentage of minority high school graduates going on to college has been declining. If these trends continue, graduate schools of education would have to enroll half or more of each year's minority graduates if minority teachers are to be found in satisfactory numbers throughout our schools — assuming few are entering by alternative routes. It is unlikely that this level of production can be attained, but the numbers make it abundantly clear that a special effort is required to make substantial progress toward this reasonable goal.

The pipeline metaphor is very apt. At each stage, greater proportions of the minority population are left behind than are whites. This would not be a problem for teaching if teaching demanded very small proportions of the college-educated population. But the reverse is true. Because teaching will need a very high proportion of college graduates in the years ahead, the problem of minority teachers cannot possibly be solved without addressing the fundamental problems of minority educational preparation throughout the pipeline.

It is essential to preserve and strengthen the compensatory education programs that assist the schools in devoting special attention and resources to children who are at risk. The commitments made since the mid-60s by federal and state governments to meet the needs of low-income and minority students must be reaffirmed. Given the promise of early childhood education for addressing the educational deficits that many children bring with them to the primary grades, all levels of government, along with community based organizations, should consider new commitments in these areas.

The Middle and Senior High Schools. The challenge at the middle and high school level is especially acute. We need to identify promising students, raise their aspirations, and support their efforts to do well in school and prepare for college.

These purposes seem best served by partnerships between schools serving poor and minority children on the one hand, and higher education institutions, employers, community based organizations and associations on the other. Programs now in existence, for example, bring Black and Hispanic engineers, mathematicians and scientists into the schools to work with individual students and groups. University partnerships provide academic and career centers and weekend and summer enrichment programs for minority students. Some college and university partnerships go farther by providing help to the school in diagnosing individual student's difficulties and designing full-year programs to help them, including study skills instruction, preparatory work for college entrance examinations, and counseling students at their school. The local business community can also open the eyes of youngsters to a whole range of career possibilities that they never knew of or never realized they might have access to. All of these programs should be strengthened and expanded.

High schools ought to take particular care in counseling poor and minority students to make certain that they do not compromise their prospects for admission to four-year colleges and universities, by virtue of the courses they select. This is especially important because the prospect of a student completing a baccalaureate program is heightened if he or she begins college as a full-time student in a four-year institution. All too often high school graduates discover after the fact that a late blooming interest in a college education cannot easily be fulfilled because of gaps in their high school academic record. While increasingly demanding state graduation requirements can help on this score, good counseling is indispensible for poor and minority youngsters who often have few others to turn to for advice.

One particularly promising development is the use on a large scale of college students to work as tutors in schools with high concentrations of low-income students. When both tutor and taught are minority students, both will benefit. Furthermore, minority college students who serve as tutors may find that they enjoy teaching sufficiently to make teaching their career choice, turning such programs into a recruiting device as well. Every state should consider emulating California in the use of college work-study funds to support the use of college students as school tutors. Institutions which have cooperative programs with industry should consider allowing students to spend a full semester working in the schools for pay or for credit.

A national program is now under development by the National Executive Service Corps to recruit from industry and the military retired people with strong mathematics and science backgrounds to serve as full-time teachers. That program could be designed to provide incentives for such people to concentrate on schools serving the poor and minorities. Bringing in retirees who are themselves members of minority groups would provide strong models of the returns on education that, in many instances, will leave a lasting impression with minority youngsters.

The Colleges and Universities. Years of effort have produced effective programs to increase the number of minorities attending and successfully completing college. They typically include pre-freshman summer program preparation, an early-warning system of potential academic problems, a high degree of interaction between faculty and students, and high expectations regarding student success. Well constructed affirmative action plans also have had a salutary effect.

If the need for minority teachers is to be met, state and institutional leaders must strengthen existing programs, develop new ones, and find the funds necessary for both.

A strong accreditation system could also help here if accrediting authorities placed a good deal of emphasis on institutional performance and practices in the area of minority student recruitment, retention and graduation.

Strengthening the Black Colleges. The

Collaboration between Queens College, the New York City Board of Education, and Louis Armstrong Middle School began in 1979 when the Board contracted with the college to help develop a model intermediate school. Since then, college faculty, student teachers, graduate interns and the college administration have been a part of the daily life of the school. Concurrently, school administrators and teachers have served as adjunct professors and guest lecturers at the college and as supervisors for student teachers.

The success of the collaboration can be seen in rising student achievement, improved attendance, increased interest in academic high school studies, and in the growing number of applications this magnet school receives each year.

The teachers' enthusiasm also shows through. "We do have more freedom than most schools to try things out educationally and that is encouraged by the administration," reports Bob Norman, the local union representative. Elizabeth Ophals, a social studies teacher, observed that, "Teachers here really sit around talking about educational practice, what might work better or how things should be done, and that makes it exciting to work here."

Louis Armstrong is a county-wide magnet school where admission is by application for children in grades 5-8. The school operates a number of innovative programs that involve both Armstrong teachers and Queens College faculty. The "Early Bird" early morning program serves 400 children with elective programs ranging from aerobics to language and is staffed by student teachers and interns from Queens.

A counseling program is staffed by counselor education interns who are graduate students at the College. College staff has helped arrange mentor programs linking students with local business people and community groups. College personnel are also involved in peer counseling, parenting classes, a community art museum, and the mainstreaming of special education students into the regular academic program.

Among the personnel who are present on a weekly basis are the associate dean, faculty who assist teachers in specific subject areas, a cadre of some 16 student teachers and a dozen graduate interns who are in the school three days a week for the entire school year. The College is as much a beneficiary of this collaboration as is the school. Associate Dean, Sydney Trubowitz, explains: "Imagine doctors never working in hospitals. The collaboration keeps us fresh. We bring in, test and come away with new ideas in a realistic setting."

Based, in part, on United Teacher, United Federation of Teachers, April 14, 1986

predominantly Black colleges enrolled only 28 percent of all Black undergraduates in 1980-81, but produced more than 48 percent of the Black education baccalaureates. These institutions make unusual efforts to reach out to Black students with marginal high school records and their programs must be strengthened.

The Task Force's proposals could make the work of Black colleges even more difficult: they will have to prepare their graduates to meet the standards set by graduate schools offering the master's degree in teaching. The states that are home to the predominantly Black institutions will need to work closely with these institutions and with the National Board for Professional Teaching Standards to help prepare graduates to meet these standards.

Improving the Rate of Community College Transfers. In the Fall of 1982, white students in community colleges constituted 36.9 percent of all whites enrolled in higher education. The figure for Blacks was 44.4 percent, and for Hispanics, 56.1 percent. Very small proportions of minorities attending two-year colleges transfer to four-year institutions, and these minority students are lost to the pool from which teachers can be selected.

Low transfer rates are an acute problem for Hispanics. However, most of the Hispanic population is concentrated in a few states, making it both possible and necessary for those states to focus particular energy on increasing the rates of transfer from their community college system to four-year programs. This requires changes both in policy and practice with respect to the purpose and curricula of these institutions. Private foundations assist in this effort, but state officials can do much to reduce this block in the pipeline. Governors, state legislators, higher education coordinating boards and college presidents need to direct their collective attention to this matter.

Financial Incentives. The need to attract minority group members into teaching is particularly great and merits a special effort on the part of public and private agencies. Individual firms could provide scholarships and fellowships to promising minorities to attend college, graduate school, or both, on the declared intention of going into teaching. The Federal government could establish national programs along the same lines. Firms and private foundations could offer challenge grants to higher education institutions, funds that would be available to support the higher education of minorities going into teaching, subject to the grant being matched by some other donor, or by the institution itself. The patterns of aid, and their variations, are well known.

What is different is the purpose. Because the Task Force has recommended that professional teacher preparation take place at the graduate level, it is particularly important that such student aid programs be focused at this level when they come into operation. Because academically proficient minority college graduates have many employment opportunities, it will be hard to attract them to teaching unless both the career itself is changed and the cost of further investment in time and money appears commensurate with the rewards such a career will offer.

Existing undergraduate student aid programs, no matter how generous, usually leave low-income students with some level of debt. They may simply be unable to pursue a teaching career, however much they may wish to do so. Student aid would make a big difference. Graduate schools of education could also greatly increase their chances of increasing minority enrollments if they notify students of awards early, perhaps in their junior year of college, subject to continued satisfactory academic performance.

The Federal government should refocus all financial aid relating to the preparation of teachers to the graduate level. If 10,000 fellowships were available each year for minority students entering Master in Teaching degree programs — with a stipulation that they serve in teaching for a specified period — a significant fraction of the 50,000 new minority teachers needed each year could be supported.

Incentives, Performance, and Productivity

Improving the professional environment for teaching will itself lead to improvements in teachers' performance. Gains, however, will be limited by present incentives that not only do not reward performance and productivity, but sometimes actually discourage them. Americans already spend more per capita on education than any other country in the free world. This plan will work only if those who must finance it are convinced that the funds are being used as efficiently as possible. Incentives for teachers must be aligned with objectives for students.

People may wonder why "lighthouse" schools, successful teaching projects and leaders who innovate are not more widely imitated. Or, perhaps even more important, why these schools, projects and leaders seem so often to flicker brightly for a moment and then settle back to the routine. The answer is simple. Altruism and pride motivate those often unnoticed teachers who extend themselves to achieve much for their students and their schools. But the system's rewards do not go to those who produce the most achievement for the students and the greatest efficiency for the taxpayer. They go to those who play the game, stay out of controversy and stand pat. That is why the examples set by the best are rarely emulated.

Consider the following. Teachers who routinely bring home students' papers and work on them late into the night are rewarded no differently from the teachers who do not. Administrators of districts with high administrative overhead suffer not at all in comparison to administrators who have figured out how to direct their resources to instructional services. Districts and schools that produce more learning in the same number of years have no reward at all. Special programs for the disadvantaged are often budgeted on the basis of children's poverty and skill levels. If the schools should succeed in raising their skills overmuch, the schools' reward would be the loss of the special funds. (Perhaps the most perverse instance of this case is classification of poorly performing low-income children as "learning disabled," a

States and school boards, working closely with teachers, should establish incentive systems that link teachers' compensation to school-wide student performance. Both administrative mechanisms and market models ought to be considered and tested.

The federal government and private foundations, should develop a substantial program of research, development, and field trials designed to improve the methods and measurement systems available for relating teachers' rewards to student progress.

Current efforts at the federal, state and local level to assess and compare student progress should pool their resources to develop common yardsticks for use by states, localities, schools and the public.

School boards and unions should work energetically to develop more collaborative ways of improving local schools. The approaches used should be directed at the search for methods of improving the professional environment for teaching while holding teachers accountable for student progress.

label that produces resources for the district, but all too often condemns the student at an early age to an academic track virtually guaranteeing future failure.) Continued receipt of the funds, of course, is in no way contingent on student progress.

There are two issues here: performance and productivity. In the first instance, the objective is the best possible performance of students. But resources are never unlimited, so we turn out to be interested in the best possible performance at the lowest possible cost. In sum: the incentives provided by the structure of schooling encourage neither better performance nor improvements in productivity.

This has, of course, been true for decades, if not longer. Why should we be so concerned now? Why should these issues turn out to be a pivot point of this report? Because we believe improvements are not likely to be made until the structure of incentives for teachers and other school employees is redesigned to reward them for student accomplishment.

But the issue is not just performance. It is also productivity. The rate at which student performance must improve exceeds by far the rate at which school revenues can reasonably be expected to rise, even at the most optimistic levels.

There is an important parallel here to the challenge faced by American business and industry. Advancing technology and the changing structure of international trade have made it imperative in recent years for American businesses exposed to foreign competition to improve productivity. That pressure shows some promise of leading to a sweeping reassessment of long-standing production methods, the introduction of new technologies, innovative labor-management practices, improved forms of organization and the introduction of new management methods — all in the search for quality and efficiency. American schools also need to produce a higher quality product with greater efficiency, but are not subject to market forces. As we have noted, educators work in a highly regulated industry that often penalizes efficiency and provides mixed incentives, at best, for improving quality.

Even if educators had strong incentives to improve performance and productivity, it is not clear that much would improve without major organizational changes. Schooling today is an overwhelmingly bureaucratic activity where, as one observer put it, "Everyone has all of the brakes and no one has any of the motors." It is unreasonable to hold teachers accountable for results when many of the important decisions about how students' needs are to be met are made by others.

To say all this is not to fault professional educators. They have as great a reserve of altruism as exists in any field. It is to suggest that improved teacher performance and productivity awaits changes in the system within which they work. What is wanted is a system that does not have to depend so heavily on altruism, one that provides more rewards for superior performance and where there are real consequences for failure.

While some educators discuss the pros and cons of contracting out for educational services one local school district superintendent has turned the idea on its head and has developed a plan for "contracting-in." Jim Walker, superintendent of North Branch Public Schools 45 miles north of Minneapolis-St. Paul, made a proposal to two teachers in the local elementary school. The proposal, to be implemented in the fall of l986, essentially puts the teachers in control of budgeting for and providing an instructional program for 90 fourth graders in one school in the North Branch School District.

The teachers find it attractive because it broadens their professional responsibilities and affords them an opportunity to define support services that will suit their needs. Each student comes with $633—the amount remaining after certain fixed costs (transportation, facilities, and the teachers' salaries) are extracted. The $633 per student or $57,000 collectively can be spent at the teachers' discretion (teacher aides, computers, field trips, or specialist services). While the Superintendent and the two teachers wanted to move teacher salaries from the fixed to the discretionary part of their budget, state law has constrained this option. So far, the two teachers have made their first decision; they opted to have a third full-time teacher be involved.

Such a system will not emerge from more extensive, more detailed or more draconian mandates. In recent years, some state legislatures, in their frustration with the perceived poor performance of the schools, have yielded to the temptation to specify in ever greater detail not only what educators are to accomplish, but how they are to go about it — the curriculum, texts, methods to be employed, and so on. The education code for some states is now printed in 10 or more volumes. To these commands are added the policies of school boards, the instructions of school district officials and the wishes of parents. Though some would say that this weight of commands frees teachers and principals to do whatever they wish, the truth is otherwise.

It is this welter of rules that produces the situation in which ". . . everyone has all of the brakes and no one has any of the motors," that makes even worse the already heavily bureaucratic environment teachers must endure. In these circumstances, teachers, in particular, cannot be expected to approach the task with renewed energy. They have many means at their disposal to frustrate legislative intent and bureaucratic pressure. It is unlikely that policymakers are better judges of the best means to improve the education of individual children than teachers. Legislation cannot make teachers effective, nor can administrative bureaucracies in large districts. Both should seek to create conditions under which it is in the direct interest of teachers and principals to do everything possible to be effective and to help their colleagues be effective.

In the public sector, as in business and industry, there are essentially only two possible approaches to the improvement of performance and productivity: administrative — or management — methods and the "unseen hand" of market mechanisms. Both depend heavily for their success on good information about performance and products being available, in the first case to managers, in the second instance to consumers. These approaches are not contradictory. In the private sector, the market disciplines the firm (and sometimes whole industries), while administrative methods are used within the firm to gain success in the market. In the public sector, one can choose administrative methods, market mechanisms, or a combination of both.

In the following sections, we outline first an administrative approach to the improvement of teachers' performance and productivity, then several possible market approaches. That is followed by a proposal related to the issue of measurement. We go on to discuss the merits of using capital investment — in information technology in particular — to improve productivity. And conclude with a discussion of the need for a new approach to labor-management issues in the schools.

There are many ways to confront these issues. We can recommend none with complete confidence because none has yet been developed with the necessary care and stood the trial of extended use in the schools. Furthermore, different approaches will appeal to different communities. What is crucial is that a start be made, that the states, the schools, and teachers recognize the importance of properly structured incentives and develop policies that make it more likely that performance and productivity will improve steadily.

An Administrative Approach. Administrative solutions require clarity about goals while providing as much freedom to the school leadership team as possible to attain those goals, and putting in place incentives to reward success and penalize failure.

Without clear priorities, failure is ensured. If states and districts want improved performance, their policymakers must spell out a limited number of clear goals and eliminate less important existing requirements. Insofar as possible, measurements of school and student performance should be used to assess progress toward stated goals for students. Measurements should not be limited to standardized achievement tests. They should include such yardsticks as rates of attendance, dropping out, job placement, and college acceptance. While standardized tests of basic skills and the acquisition of facts have their uses, they need to take second place to more sophisticated measures of a range of higher order cognitive processes.

It is essential for teachers to participate in setting goals at the local level, deciding how to assess student progress, developing compensation systems, and other matters related to effective performance. Parents should also be part of this process of goal setting. Once goals are decided, school staff should have as much freedom as possible in determining how they will be met.

Accountability should go considerably beyond the typical approach of simply publishing performance results. The Task Force encourages experimentation and additional research to explore ways that school staffs which produce outstanding gains in student performance can receive substantial benefit from that increase in productivity — including increased compensation. These efforts should build on sound education principles. For this reason it is particularly important in a school setting to emphasize and reward the entire staff for student progress. First, because the contribution of individual teachers to student progress is extremely difficult to measure and, second, because it is important to provide strong incentives to the staff to work as a team on behalf of the students.

The goals that are set for the school must reflect state and local goals and standards as well as parents' wishes for their children. But it is very important that they also be structured to reflect what teachers think they can achieve, because, if this is not done, they will have little commitment to their achievement. One way to do this was described in the scenario presented earlier in this report. If teachers' rewards depend on the achievement of the students, then the amount of the rewards can be keyed to the degree to which teachers set high goals and achieve them. If low goals are set, then low rewards can be expected. Conversely, achievement of ambitious goals should bring high rewards. A structure of this sort would establish a good basis for constructive dialogue between a school's faculty and the school board, one in

The idea for contracting-in originally developed as a spinoff of a mini-grant proposal submitted by a teacher on staff. The superintendent and teachers have been planning the experiment for almost a year. Several important issues have been worked out. Parents will elect to have their children participate in the program, which means the teachers will have to market their plan as one of several instructional options already available in this school.

The educational program and the curriculum are well defined. The students must attain the specified outcomes, but how they do that is up to the teachers. The continuation of their program will depend upon their ability to attract and retain students. An informal support system is in place to assist the teachers if they need it. The superintendent is available for consultation and will sign off on all budget purchases. The elementary school principal will also play an informal consulting role.

Superintendent Walker believes it is an idea that, if successful, might prove attractive to groups of teachers who want to have more responsibility and authority over their instructional program than teaching typically offers. It is his hope that it will also prevent some teachers from leaving the school district.

"In an adjacent room, I found another group of fourth grade students. They were very busy making things with LEGO stuff. But this was no ordinary LEGO set. In addition to the familiar building block modules, there were various kinds of sensors that could be built into the constructions and electric motors that could be mounted on them to impart a dizzying variety of types of motion. The sensors and the motors could be connected by the children to a computer that, in turn, made it possible for the children to use data coming from the sensors to control the motion of the things they built out of the LEGO parts.

"This was the design workshop. In it, boys and girls learned more math and science and technology by the fourth grade level than I had ever thought possible. Consider the car that followed the adhesive tape. The instruction to the computer was in form of: if the value returned by the sensor is equal to or less than x, then turn b degrees to the right; if, having maintained this direction for a specified interval the value returned by the sensor does not increase above the specified value, turn so many degrees to the left and so on.

which both will try to set high goals, but in a realistic context.

The students themselves are an essential feature of that context. While we must have high expectations for all students, if the characteristics of the students are not taken into account in the design of programs to encourage increased performance and productivity, the effect will be to drive the best teachers out of schools serving the students most in need of their services.

We should be particularly clear on one point. No method that we know of for measuring student performance and connecting it to teachers' rewards is yet satisfactory. This is not surprising, since little effort has thus far gone into development of such methods, and much is required. There is no reason in principle why satisfactory systems for this purpose cannot be developed, but none will work as designed unless states, local authorities and the teachers work together to define systems that meet their collective needs.

Inevitably, there will be some schools with performance so far below a reasonable standard that strong intervention is required. Schools with consistently substandard performance should receive technical assistance from the district and possibly the state. If substandard performance persists, the leadership team should be replaced.

A Market Approach. Market methods could also produce incentives for improved performance and productivity. Markets have proven to be very efficient instruments to allocate

resources and motivate people in many sectors of American life. They can also make it possible for all public school students to gain equal access to school resources. Though such models should only be introduced when careful planning has assured that the rights of all students will be protected, the potential for improvement in teacher performance and productivity that might be derived from market approaches to public school education is considerable.

There are a number of ways market approaches could be introduced in a school district. Some options are:

- Creation of specialty schools with enrollments drawn from throughout the district.

- Open enrollment among all public schools of a district could permit teachers and principals to develop very different schools. All schools would be equally accessible and the market would determine their viability.

- Open enrollment could be extended across district lines. Students would take their local, state and federal funds with them, creating incentives for districts, as well as schools, to perform well and compete for their clientele.

These approaches should be used only when there are policies in place to preclude racial or ethnic segregation, to ensure that there are no artificial barriers created that impeded any student's opportunity to attend the school of his or her choice, and to assure that students who do not exercise their option to leave their neighborhood school do not suffer as a result.

- Board-certified teachers might collaborate to offer their services for hire to the professional teachers responsible for a school, taking responsibility for anything from an individual course to an entire area of the curriculum. School faculties looking to expand their offerings or strengthen a particular weakness in the faculty might find such an arrangement particularly attractive.

- Similarly, once appropriate incentive and accountability structures were in place, Lead Teachers might find it in their best interest to contract for some of the services they need, holding service providers, such as testing firms and computer service vendors, responsible for providing high quality services at the lowest possible cost.

Improving Measurement Tools. Whatever approach is taken to the improvement of performance and productivity, good yardsticks of student progress are needed that permit the comparison of performance in different settings and that can easily be grasped by the public.

The resistance by many teachers to performance-oriented incentive systems is, quite appropriately, based on the inadequacy of available measures. The most widely used standardized tests measure a very narrow range of behaviors, and little has been done to construct efficient and valid measures of the types of achievement related to higher cognitive functions that were most strongly emphasized earlier in this report. Moreover,

many non-cognitive measures, such as dropout rates, have not been standardized, making legitimate comparisons impossible.

Progress in this arena is very important. It will take time and will be expensive. It will require substantial support from the federal government and private foundations for programs of research, development and field trials. Current efforts at the national, state and local levels to assess and compare student progress are encouraging, but there is much to be gained by pooling resources to develop common yardsticks which could then be applied by states, localities and schools as they see fit. Here the Task Force has in mind, among others, the work of the Council of Chief State School Officers' new Assessment Center and the extension of the National Assessment of Educational Progress to permit cross-state comparisons.

It is also true that agreement on common metrics involves technical issues but is not only a technical matter. The states, teachers and other members of the education community, as well as representatives of at-risk students, all have an interest in the way that widely used metrics are defined. All need to be involved, therefore, in their definition.

The time seems ripe: there is much stronger interest in reporting comparative data on student progress than at any time in recent memory.

Technology and Productivity. If the proposals we make to create a professional environment for teaching are adopted, teachers and students will be able to make more effective

"There are many observations that could be made about this lab, but one is irresistible. It is apparently true of all the design labs of this sort that the girls take to the work at least as readily as the boys. Bear in mind that what is being given in this lab is a class in engineering, a first exposure to the pleasures of equipment design, in which the participants are exposed to the uses of mathematics and science in a way that is clearly enthralling."

Marc Tucker, Executive Director, Carnegie Forum, testimony to the National Governors Association on Hennigan Elementary School, Boston, January, 1986. The school works collaboratively with Seymour Papert and his colleagues at the Massachusetts Institute of Technology.

use of technology, thereby increasing the schools' productivity.

In general, today's microcomputers have a very limited capacity as teachers, but they can make possible student gains in crucial areas of the curriculum that might be very difficult to achieve otherwise. All over the country students are using the power of the computer to learn things and accomplish tasks that few believed possible for people of their age.

Fourth graders in some low-income communities use microcomputers to write competent essays and produce computer animated art. One inner-city elementary school's students are learning basic engineering principles as they design and build computer-controlled experiments. Middle school students are learning the principles of advanced mathematics as they write programs to create complex geometric shapes. High school students are learning how to use spreadsheet software designed for business to optimize feeding schedules for individual dairy cows on their family farms, thereby achieving efficiencies that have eluded their parents.

Currently available software also makes it possible for music students to compose, edit, and play music for multiple instruments. Science students can set up remote data-gathering stations and connect them to microcomputers to forecast the weather in remote mountain valleys, learning both about the science of weather forecasting and the principles of computer-based modeling. Students in technical high schools can use

microcomputer-based tools to master sophisticated project- and budget-planning techniques for use in the construction trades.

None of these subjects is taught by the computer, but the computer is used by the student as a tool to accomplish these tasks. The result is that students of all ability levels can learn much more, and learn it earlier in their school career.

Video recorders and laser disk players are now available that can bring large amounts of information to individual students on demand, including high quality visual images.

The prospects are fascinating. These technologies should make it possible to relieve teachers of much of the burden of imparting information to students, thereby freeing them for coaching, diagnosing learning difficulties, developing students' creative and problem-solving capacities and participating in school management.

Though it is possible to adapt these technologies to conventional classrooms in which all students are doing the same thing at the same time, they are far better used in environments in which students as individuals or in small groups work on the machines pursuing their own goals in their own ways.

The substantial productivity advances that can be expected from computer use will result not from replacing teachers with machines, but through greatly improved achievement by students when good teachers are augmented by properly used technology.

Labor-Management Relations. At the heart of this report is a set of recommendations intended to create a professional environment for teaching in schools and districts. It will be impossible to approach that objective unless teachers, administrators and school boards join together in the effort to make it happen. That is why, throughout this report, we have spoken of the need for local policymakers to actively involve teachers in the design of new arrangements.

In many, if not most cases, involving teachers means working through their representatives, the unions. The confrontational stance that frequently characterizes the relationship between school boards and unions could doom these recommendations.

We have found school districts in the United States that have already moved a long way toward implementation of some of the proposals made here. In some cases, they served as the inspiration for those proposals. Almost without exception, those programs resulted from the constructive actions of labor and management working collaboratively.

Both sides need to try hard to overcome a legacy of conflict and confrontation. Both boards and unions have made major contributions to the welfare of teachers and the performance of schools as collective bargaining became a widespread feature of the education landscape. They will continue to do so. But the focus of bargaining can and should be changed. Unions, boards, and school administrators need to work out a new accommodation based on exchanging professional-level salaries and a professional environment, on the one hand, for the acceptance of professional standards of excellence and the willingness to be held fully accountable for the results of one's work, on the other.

Taxpayers and the larger society have an obvious stake in the success of measures taken to enhance school performance and productivity. The interest of education professionals in these matters is no less great, because their ability to get the resources they need to do the job depends on demonstrated performance and effective use of available resources.

Teacher Salaries and Benefits

Every occupation presents its own pattern of rewards and incentives. Starting salaries and average salaries, the distribution of salaries within the occupation, and the average time it takes to move to various plateaus along the salary scale all influence the behavior of both prospective candidates for entry into the occupation and those already employed in the occupation. Until quite recently, medicine paid very modest salaries to beginning MDs, but it attracted and held very capable people because, in part, the prospect of very high earnings exists for the large majority of physicians after their period of apprenticeship. Accountants' compensation patterns look different from that of doctors, promising good wages earlier in the career and simultaneously holding open the opportunity of high wages for those who become partners in public accounting firms.

Entering, average, and the range of teachers' salaries should be increased to levels adequate to attract and retain teachers of high academic ability.

Continuing education credits should no longer be used as a basis of salary determination. Teacher compensation systems should be based on the following attributes:

1. Job Function — Level of responsibility.

2. Competence — As determined by level of Board certification.

3. Seniority — Experience in the classroom.

4. Productivity — Contribution to improved student performance.

The teacher's contribution to student performance is the hardest of these attributes to assess. Performance-based compensation systems should be regarded as developmental and teachers should participate actively in their design.

States and districts should move to eliminate the obstacles to career mobility for teachers.

States and localities should use pay incentives to assure an equitable distribution of teachers among high priority schools and school districts.

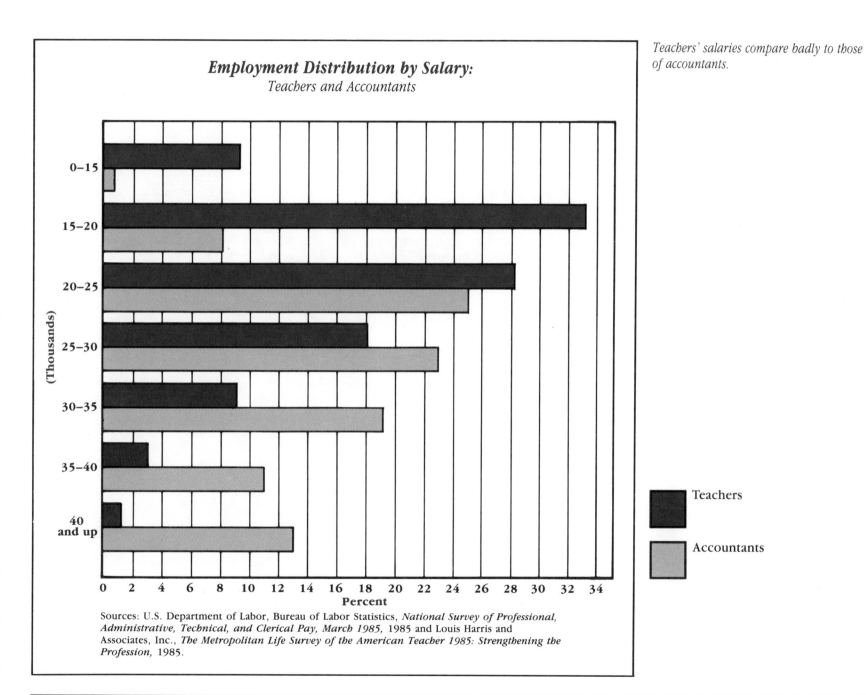

Employment Distribution by Salary:
Teachers and Accountants

Teachers' salaries compare badly to those of accountants.

(Thousands)

0–15

15–20

20–25

25–30

30–35

35–40

40 and up

0 2 4 6 8 10 12 14 16 18 20 22 24 26 28 30 32 34

Percent

■ Teachers

▨ Accountants

Sources: U.S. Department of Labor, Bureau of Labor Statistics, *National Survey of Professional, Administrative, Technical, and Clerical Pay, March 1985,* 1985 and Louis Harris and Associates, Inc., *The Metropolitan Life Survey of the American Teacher 1985: Strengthening the Profession,* 1985.

Such compensation patterns attract a cadre of very capable people who move into leadership positions in their professions while continuing their practice and acquiring increasing responsibilities and pay. The profession thus holds onto its best people.

The situation in teaching is far different. Teaching is a high turnover, early exit occupation. Working conditions leave much to be desired. The typical salary schedule puts teaching, as a career, at an extraordinary disadvantage if it hopes to compete for the best young people with other professions. Teachers' starting salaries are at the low end of the spectrum for college graduates and the prospects for salary growth do not compare with other occupations.

Teacher salaries are extraordinarily compressed when compared to other occupations demanding a college degree. They start low and remain low. Most teachers approach the top of the scale within 10 to 12 years after entering the work force. Teachers find themselves in their mid-thirties faced with the prospect of no salary growth in real terms when their peers are beginning to enter their prime earning years. It is small wonder then that half of all teachers leave the work force within seven years and that the caliber of new teachers entering the schools does not compare favorably with college graduates entering other fields. The salary structure impels able teachers, those most likely to raise the performance levels of the schools, to leave the profession just as they acquire the experience to assume effective leadership.

A recently released survey of former

teachers demonstrates the effects: only one percent of teachers reported incomes of $40,000 or more in 1984; but 15 percent of those who left teaching in the last five years had such earnings. While 32 percent of the ex-teachers had earnings of $20,000 or less, 42 percent of current teachers reported such incomes. At the same time, former teachers appear satisfied with their health and retirement benefits. They report less job stress, greater control over their own work, and increased job satisfaction. Eighty-three percent of former teachers said they were unlikely to return to the classroom, suggesting that new policies to hold on to our most able teachers may be more effective than trying to entice former teachers back to the classroom.

The modest incomes of teachers relative to the income of others is not universal among industrial countries. When the salaries of Japanese teachers are compared to those of their countrymen, they turn out to be 37 percent higher than those of American teachers when compared to all American workers. If teachers at the top of the scale are compared, the Japanese teachers' advantage exceeds 80 percent.

Under current compensation practices, seniority and the accumulation of graduate credits determine the outcome. Compare this with the rewards and recognition for above average performance that can be found in professional practice partnerships in architecture or the law. The successful architect can not only look forward to a larger paycheck, but to more challenging and demanding commissions. Young attorneys with satisfied clients can expect their client base to expand

and their prospects of being offered a partnership to increase.

These examples cannot be written off as irrelevant simply because education is, for the most part, a public service not amenable to market forces. Compensation policies that create a set of positive incentives for excellence can be found within public education. One has to look no farther than the state college or university to find such arrangements in faculty salary schedules.

Current practice in elementary and secondary education is also frequently defended on the grounds that to differentiate between teachers in compensation will only work to undermine the need for active collaboration and colleagueship among teachers. Once again the careful observer need only look at physicians with varying levels of pay and expertise consulting with one another on a particular case, or junior and senior members of law and accounting firms working together as a team to address the special needs of each client, to quickly become convinced that the underlying argument against linking teacher pay to teacher quality runs aground on the facts.

While quality and compensation need to be connected, just how a school district goes about this can make a vast difference in the outcomes achieved. The Task Force believes that it is possible to do this badly or to do it well, the difference hinging on design and execution. It is, therefore, important that as states and local school districts begin to consider reorienting their teacher salary policies

attention is paid to the following key principles.

Competitive Salaries. Teaching must offer salaries, benefits and working conditions competitive with those of other professions. Assuming that a better than average level of intellectual ability is desired in the teaching work force, the schools will be competing for talent with a wide range of enterprises that, in many instances, are prepared to bid up salaries until they get the people they believe they need to prosper as an organization.

To attract such people, districts will have to pay salaries at least equal to those offered in the mid-range of the wage scale for occupations requiring comparable education, roughly equivalent to what accountants are paid today.

Salaries need not become fully competitive overnight, but a start in this direction must be made immediately. A message should go out to prospective and current teachers that the profession can anticipate steadily rising economic rewards. It should also be understood that just raising average pay will be a very inefficient use of new dollars if not accompanied by a fundamental restructuring of teacher compensation policies.

The task of finding the funds for competitive salaries falls to local school boards and to the city, county and municipal governments responsible for school district budgets. These jurisdictions also need the support and cooperation of the state to balance disparities in tax capacity between local jurisdictions. State government can also help make salaries

An illustration of how the mid-points on a hypothetical teacher salary schedule in an "average" American community might compare to the average earnings for the six categories of non-managing accountants established by the Bureau of Labor Statistics. The BLS categories are based on level of responsibility and experience (the higher the category the more responsible the position). The Task Force example displays two numbers for the first three categories: the second number is the average annual salary for teachers on 10-month contracts: the first, the equivalent full year salary.

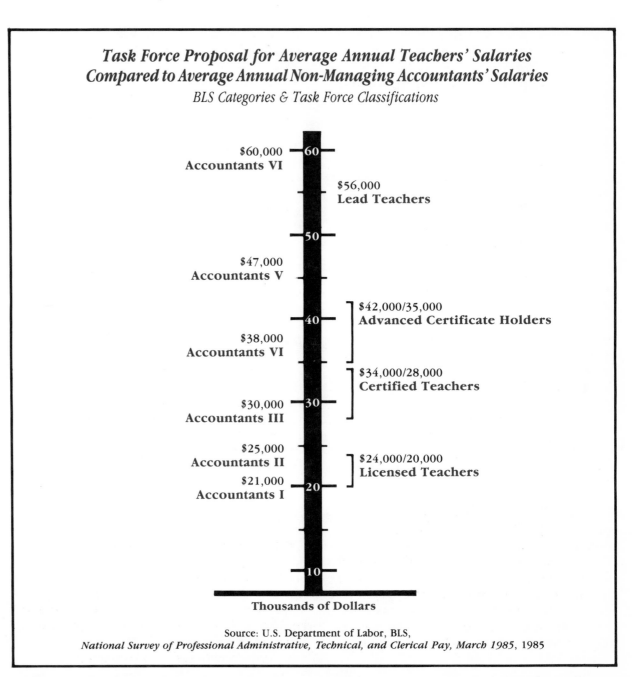

Task Force Proposal for Average Annual Teachers' Salaries Compared to Average Annual Non-Managing Accountants' Salaries

BLS Categories & Task Force Classifications

$60,000
Accountants VI

$56,000
Lead Teachers

$47,000
Accountants V

$42,000/35,000
Advanced Certificate Holders

$38,000
Accountants VI

$34,000/28,000
Certified Teachers

$30,000
Accountants III

$25,000
Accountants II

$24,000/20,000
Licensed Teachers

$21,000
Accountants I

Thousands of Dollars

Source: U.S. Department of Labor, BLS,
National Survey of Professional Administrative, Technical, and Clerical Pay, March 1985, 1985

more competitive by establishing minimum starting salaries at levels significantly in excess of current practice. Barring full state assumption of education finance, however, salaries will be determined mainly at the local level.

Restructured Salary Schedules. Current salary schedules recognize only years in service and graduate credits. The Task Force believes that schools need to move toward compensation systems based on the following dimensions:

- Job Function - with a restructured work force, teachers ought to be assigned to different salary schedules based on their level of responsibility.

- Level of Certification - establishment of a professional certification board will provide an equitable basis for recognizing demonstrated competence in teaching.

- Seniority - experience in the classroom provides intangible benefits not captured by the most sophisticated assessment processes and deserves recognition.

- Productivity - compensation policies must reward teacher contributions to improved student performance and take into account the inability to demonstrate such improvements. As we noted earlier, we value incentives provided to entire school staffs particularly highly, and we believe that significant improvements must be made to performance-oriented compensation systems before they can be widely used.

The Task Force believes that teachers themselves, along with state and local school officials, are best able to define these structures, but the dimensions outlined above should drive salary growth and career advancement.

The teacher's contribution to student performance is the hardest of these attributes to assess. In order to speed the use of such measures, the federal government and private foundations should sponsor a series of targeted research activities to advance the state-of-the-art in school performance measures.

New categories will mean little unless real differences in pay are associated with the new classification scheme. The range of most current salary scales is very limited. Significant salary increments must be associated with different levels of responsibility. Such a development will promote a teaching force eager for additional responsibility and willing to pursue the Advanced Teacher's certificate, whether or not they wish to become Lead Teachers.

Taking the current salary structure of non-managing accountants reported by the Bureau of Labor Statistics as a guidepost, the Task Force has developed two hypothetical salary structures designed to illustrate what teacher pay might eventually look like if school districts adopted the general principles laid out above. Two examples have been prepared to reflect the diversity in pay practices across the country that are likely to persist, as teachers salaries will continue to be sensitive to prevailing wage rates which differ markedly from community to community.

However one looks at these figures, it should be obvious that this plan calls for teacher compensation systems that will represent a significant departure from current practice for almost every school district in the nation. The figures below are set at 10 percent above and 10 percent below what the national average salaries might be for teachers in each category and are stated in constant dollar terms.

	District I	District II
Lead Teachers holding Advanced Certificates, 12 months employment	$42,000 - 59,000	$52,000 - 72,000
Advanced Certificate holders who are not Lead Teachers, 10-month contract	$26,000 - 38,000	$31,000 - 46,000
Certified Teachers, the majority of the teaching force, 10-month contract	$19,000 - 32,000	$23,000 - 39,000
Licensed Teachers prior to Certification, 10-month contract	$15,000 - 21,000	$18,000 - 25,000

In each instance the salary range reflects the pay differential for teachers with more or less time in grade.

To the extent localities share the Task Force's view on the importance of competitive salaries, both more and less expensive variations are likely to evolve. Regional labor markets also will exert an important influence on the actual rates of pay each school district offers. Local boards and state authorities need to understand that the market for teachers is changing. Rising de-mand for teachers will create much greater competition for especially capable teachers. In an economy that values well-educated workers even more than is true today, all employers will face stiffer competition for tomorrow's college graduates, and school districts will have to live with that reality as they seek more capable teachers.

Increased Mobility. No national market exists for teachers. This makes teaching a less attractive occupation than many others and contributes to the number of able teachers who leave the classroom each year.

Most states certify and license teachers upon graduation from an approved course of study at in-state institutions. Although reciprocity agreements are common, teachers moving from one state to another often experience serious difficulties establishing their credentials anew.

Local district hiring rules and state retirement system regulations also create problems. Many districts limit the number of years of experience credited to a new teacher. This holds down costs. But such policies limit mobility and in many instances drive good people out of the profession.

State retirement systems to which most elementary and secondary teachers belong exact severe penalties if a school teacher relocates. Vesting rules typically require 5 to 10 years of service before a teacher can have access to the funds that have been placed in their account. "Purchase of credit" rules often require a teacher to make up both employer and employee's contribution if they desire the number of years credit in the new system that they had earned in the old.

The notion of relocating to obtain a promotion is completely foreign to elementary and secondary school teachers. Moving from firm to firm in search of greater responsibility and compensation is taken for granted by most college graduates and such mobility is a fairly efficient process for matching talent with new employment opportunities. If professional environments for teaching are adopted on a wide scale throughout the country, they will create a new set of incentives for teacher relocation. Current artificial barriers to teacher mobility must be dismantled as part of an effort to create a free and efficient teacher labor market.

A More Equitable Distribution of Teachers. Current education financing arrangements make it possible for the wealthiest districts to attract a disproportionate share of the best teachers. Within districts, the most experienced teachers are often assigned to the most promising students. Incentives at every level should be designed to ensure that the students most in need of help are taught by many of the best and most experienced teachers. Three points bearing directly on the question of inequities in the distribution of talented teachers deserve comment.

First, grant funds should be available to provide promising low-income and minority students pursuing the Master in Teaching degree with financial support in exchange for service as a teacher for a fixed period of time following graduation. This service should be rendered in schools designated as high priority by the states.

Second, states should consciously promote the equitable distribution of talented teachers by offering salary supplements to certified teachers in high-need districts. This can be accomplished by providing funds exclusively for teacher salaries to districts serving high-need students, and by designing other policies to encourage fairer distribution of the most able teachers.

Third, the districts themselves should offer incentives to experienced teachers to teach in high priority schools. These incentives could come in the form of additional pay, greater support staffing, and improved physical conditions. Incentive pay combined with real improvements in working conditions appears to be the most feasible solution to this problem.

Implementing the Plan

Implementing the Plan

Paying for Quality

The cost of implementing these proposals over time is substantial. For the nation as a whole, however, there is ample precedent for new investment in education on the scale called for by this report. The country has a history of meeting educational crises head on. New institutions have been created, old methods replaced, and fresh dollars committed. Similar determination is necessary to address the teacher quality crisis.

To make this come about, the public must be convinced that the returns on this new investment in education promise to be tangible and that the policy changes advocated in this report set the stage for major long-term improvement of America's competitive position in world markets, for wider participation in an expanding economy across the social spectrum, and for a better educated citizenry capable of preserving democracy well into the 21st century.

The incremental cost of the reform must be weighed in relation to the cost of inaction and the returns in productivity.

Maintaining the status quo will not cost much less than the true incremental costs of this plan. Expenditures will inevitably rise as enrollments swell. The cost calculations below consider both the expense for qualitative improvements and the real expense confronting schools as enrollments rise. A status quo budget will produce a substantial decline in teacher quality and student accomplishment as the shrinking number of bachelor's degree holders find

better markets for their services. It follows then that if schools do not make more attractive job offers, the quality of new teachers will decline. The country, therefore, does not enjoy the luxury of deciding whether or not to spend more; it must decide how much more to spend and how best to spend it.

Capturing the Benefits of Productivity.
Improving the rate of return on our current investment in education requires additional investment. Greater revenues are required because education is a highly labor intensive enterprise heavily dependent on the quality and performance of the teaching force. Organizing and managing this resource in different ways will make more productive use of both the talented individuals already in our schools and those we are able to attract to teaching.

The professionalization of the teacher work force is the key. Professionalization promises much greater returns on our investment by reorienting policy to enhance the productivity of teachers. The effect would be to lower the cost of attracting more capable people to the classroom. In the long run, in schools as in business, the cost of quality is negative.

The plan also makes it necessary to shift resources from administrative overhead to instruction. There are probably far greater opportunities for resource reallocation in large districts than in small. Large central office bureaucracies not only have reserved to themselves a broad range of decisionmaking authority that should be reassigned to schools, but have also managed to capture a growing share of local resources. One measure of the opportunity for reallocating resources has been the shift during the last 10 years of the share of school district budgets devoted to teachers' salaries: down to 40 percent of expenditures from 49 percent in a very short period of time.

A system that is much more productive and efficient also promises a host of cost savings that may not be so immediately obvious. Most striking is the promise of students progressing faster in their studies and learning more than they now do in any given period of time. There are many ways to capture the benefit of such improved performance.

One is to compress the total time spent in formal education before young adults enter the work force. Another is reductions in the cost of remediation in high school and college. But most important are the reductions of the costs of dependency and the great increase that would result in the productivity of the general economy as better educated graduates join the work force.

The Task Force's proposals, while initially increasing costs, should also foster a gradual reduction in outlays for teacher education. The establishment of teaching as a profession should not only bring more capable people to the schools, but significantly extend the average life of a teaching career, which now sees half of each new teacher cohort leave the schools within seven years after taking their first job. Savings in the cost of teacher education as turnover and retirement rates fall and the demand for new teachers diminishes would gradually help offset the cost of increased salaries needed both to draw and hold good people.

Steadily Rising Revenues. However large the savings generated by increasing productivity, there is no question that the Task Force proposals for more competitive teachers salaries will, over time, call for increased state and local revenues. Governors, state legislators and local school boards will be faced with a genuine challenge. It is not, however, unprecedented. During the past 15 years, a period of declining enrollments, the public has supported a real increase of 32 percent in school revenues. During the 1950s and 1960s, as the schools attempted to absorb the "baby boom" generation, real revenues rose 120 percent and 108 percent respectively.

Recent increases in education spending have come during a period when the economy has been quite mixed, growing at an average annual rate in real terms of 2.7 percent. It does not seem unreasonable to expect that over the next 10 to 15 years similar moderate rates of economic growth can be achieved, in which case an expanding economy can provide the fuel to finance this plan.

Education will be competing with other legitimate claims on the public treasury. Therefore, it is important to note that the recommendations taken together do not amount to a greater claim on national resources than the current proportion of the gross national product devoted to the schools. Our estimates of the incremental costs to fund this reform package suggest that an average annual real increase of resources on the order of 2.8 percent per year over a period of 10 years, or 1.9 percent over 15 years, would be sufficient.

These estimates rest on an analysis of the national cost of operating elementary and secondary schools that resemble the schools described in the text. Two factors dominate the new cost structure: the shift to competitive teachers salaries and the large influx of support personnel to assist teachers. Gradually increasing teacher pay and establishing a salary structure with incentives to remain in the profession accounts for the largest share of incremental costs. The cost of operating a larger teaching staff as enrollments increase and providing salary increases enabling teachers to keep pace with a rising standard of living over a 10-15 year implementation period, adds significantly to the bill.

Support personnel costs are a smaller part of additional expense, while the added cost of tutors and other instructional aides is fairly minimal.

During the 1950s and 1960s elementary and secondary education revenues increased in real terms at average annual rates of 7 and 8 percent. The past 15 years, though, have witnessed average annual increases of only 1.9 percent. The estimates we have made of the incremental cost of transforming the schools and teaching along the lines laid out in the report, suggest that if we were willing to wait 15 years, and revenues grew at the same rate during this period as they have in the last 15 years, enough new money will

have been raised to pay this bill. However, the policy context in which this report has been written suggests that the nation cannot afford such a leisurely pace.

The window of opportunity that exists to address the teacher quality problem argues instead for setting 10 years as the target. The requirement of real annual revenue increments of 2.8 percent over 10 years is very close to the economy's performance of 2.7 percent average annual growth during the past 15 years. This has not been a period of extraordinary economic performance by the United States. Hence, with modest expectations for economic growth, expectations consistent with recent experience, our plan can be funded with education spending that simply maintains education's current share of GNP. What is required is political leadership over the long haul, through good economies and bad, to achieve such progress.

In sum, a growing economy will pay for this plan providing education is allowed to keep even with the economy. This has not been our recent history. Financing this plan then calls for a change in priorities. We must shift from the policy of giving education a declining percentage of GNP to letting it keep up.

This requirement for greater investment will vary from jurisdiction to jurisdiction and does not have to be met all at once. At the outset an accident of demography helps. The sharp upturn in teacher retirements, which is partly responsible for the growing divergence between teacher supply and demand, will generate, fairly immediately, a positive cash flow as teachers at the top of the salary scale leave the school payroll and are replaced with teachers further down the schedule. By gradually adjusting salaries upward and simultaneously changing the basic structure of compensation plans, turnover will moderate and a signal will be broadcast that a teaching career now promises much more in the way of genuine rewards in salary and satisfaction.

Equalizing Purchasing Power. Plans to raise new revenues for education always raise difficult issues of equity. Local districts have very uneven capacities to raise revenues, and some states have meager tax bases to support the entire range of public services they must provide.

In a new world of Board-certified teachers and shortages of teaching talent, low-wealth states and districts will be at a substantial disadvantage. The result, if nothing else changes, will be that the current maldistribution of teaching talent will become quite obvious for all to see. State departments of education will be able to pinpoint where such teachers are clustered and where they are hard to find. The relationship between district wealth, tax effort and teacher quality will be easy to discern.

It can be seen today in the practice of high-salary districts raiding the best young teachers from low-salary districts once they have gained some experience in the classroom. The latter districts, in effect, provide a training service for the former districts and see the returns on their investment captured by others.

Not only do such districts suffer from diminished teacher capacity, but the breadth and depth of their instructional program is often compromised. School districts that cannot find or hold science teachers and choose not to have English teachers monitor chemistry labs, regularly scale back their science offerings. Localities that cannot attract mathematics teachers concentrate those that remain in algebra and geometry, and students with an interest in tackling more advanced math find such coursework unavailable.

Some progress has been made on these issues during the past 15 years. But in most states sharp disparities in revenue raising capacity between school districts remain and state education financing formulas only partially address these problems.

If all children are to get a fair opportunity to be taught by Board-certified teachers, governors and state legislators need to ensure that new state funds for education are allocated to localities through equalization formulas that take account of at least three central factors — the district's tax base, the composition of the district's student population, and local wage rates. In some instances special allowances also have to be made for large urban areas that have a disproportionate share of dependent citizens without a commensurate flow of revenues to meet their needs.

The federal government also has a role to play in addressing interstate disparities. In the sellers market that is forecast, greater mobility will have the salutary effect of providing especially promising teacher candidates and Board-certified teachers with much brighter prospects for landing a rewarding job than has previously been the case. While such a market may be attractive for talented teachers, poor states may be in for a difficult time. The federal government should consider leveling the playing field by adopting the model of general purpose equalization grants long accepted by many other Western democracies with federal forms of government (e.g., Australia, Canada and the Federal Republic of Germany). In these nations the central government makes grants to the states and provinces to ensure that jurisdictions with weak revenue bases have adequate resources to provide essential public services.

The Task Force recognizes that the federal government's current fiscal circumstances make immediate action along such lines highly improbable. However, the proposals advanced in this report will not be implemented overnight. In the longer term, such initiatives would make good policy sense on economic grounds and be very consistent with the long term federal commitment to equal educational opportunity.

An Open Invitation to Join in the Work Ahead

Countless people who were never at the table can say they wrote part of this report. Implementation will have just as many authors. A great many Americans are thinking hard this year about teaching and how to strengthen it. We drew on their ideas and would like to draw on their energy and commitment to put the ideas into practice. Against that background, it doesn't make

sense for us to tell others what to do. We *can* say what we will do, and issue an open invitation to the friends of good teaching to join in the common work.

The National Board for Professional Teaching Standards. We will convene a group immediately to plan for the National Board for Professional Teaching Standards. Among the first tasks will be the creation of the Board's initial agenda. It is our view that the Board must define what teachers need to know and be able to do. It must support the creation of rigorous, valid assessments to see that certified teachers do meet those standards. We think the Board should work with the states to eliminate barriers to a truly national labor market for teachers. And it must do all of these things in concert with the profession and interested members of the public.

An Invitation to Teachers. We are convinced that teachers will support much higher standards for their profession. The evidence has accumulated steadily through surveys conducted by Metropolitan Life, the California Commission on Teaching, the National Education Association, the American Federation of Teachers, and the National Teacher Forum of the Education Commission of the States, to cite just a few. What you think about these recommendations is important. Write to your associations and to policy leaders in your state. Talk about these ideas among your colleagues and with others in your community. Participate in local efforts to strengthen school programs, both as an individual and as a member of your association. Watch for the creation of the National Board. We especially invite you to act on the belief that teaching is a complex, difficult profession by seeking Board certification when it becomes available. After you become Board certified, take advantage of your right to elect teacher representatives to the Board.

An Invitation to State Policy Leaders.
Vigorous action in the states over the last few years helped create the opportunity for this report. Many themes in this report reflect state experience. Now there is a need to reflect on what has been done and what needs to be done. We invite governors, legislators and other state policy leaders to convene panels in their own states to consider this report, as well as those from similar groups that have appeared or will appear this year. It is time to assert a renewed education agenda in the states. In particular, we are looking for a few states to lead the way in rethinking the way schools work. We invite state leaders to find local boards and educators willing to create a professional environment for teaching in the schools that is performance oriented. We invite state leaders to create the incentives and remove the obstacles to permit this to happen. We invite the foundations to join those who come forward.

We invite governors and others to lead campaigns to recruit able people to become teachers, and to create the conditions that will enable them to heed that call. The schools need minorities, former teachers, people interested in a career change, and young people selecting their first career. Each group may require a distinct recruitment strategy. All must meet high performance standards before they enter the classroom.

We invite governors and legislators to examine where the educational dollar is going. If education can retain its current share of the GNP in a growing economy, the nation could fully support the changes we recommend. We challenge political leaders in the states to match that level of support in the future, and to make sure that it goes to instruction.

An Invitation to Local Action. In the future, local communities and their representatives will determine the outcome. They can contribute a great deal if they make it clear that they value the kind of teachers who achieve Board certification. But local boards, administrators, teachers, unions and parents need not wait for the National Board for Professional Teaching Standards. They can work now for more productive and effective schools. It will mean, among other things, acceptance of union and management collaboration on educational matters as well as issues typically contained in the contract. Put simply, teachers and administrators need to talk with each other about the education of children. They have to make time for this during the school day. It will mean genuine teacher involvement in and responsibility for educational decisions. It will mean a willingness of local boards and district administrators to set high standards and then give schools and the professionals in them more leeway in deciding how to meet the standards. That entails a professional commitment on the part of teachers and principals to meet those standards.

The Opportunity for Leadership in Higher Education. In recent years, higher education has largely left school reform to the political leadership in the states. We invite leaders at the highest levels in colleges and universities to reassert the importance of educating outstanding teachers and their responsibility for doing that. It is a matter not only for deans of education but also for presidents, trustees, and the arts and sciences faculty. We applaud those who strengthen undergraduate liberal arts programs. We welcome teacher educators who set ambitious goals, and who focus not on what is but what can be.

Teacher education can meet much higher standards. We see a willingness to do so. The focus must be on what teachers need to know and be able to do. We encourage a period of intense work to develop many different ways to train candidates to meet high professional teacher standards. We encourage the same attention to the delivery of continuing education to veteran teachers. While half of the teachers in this decade will be new to the classroom, half are already there. Their skills, like the skills of any professional, require continual renewal.

An Invitation to Students. We invite you to consider a career in teaching. As America rises to the challenge we have laid out here — and we have no doubt that it will — there will be no career more rewarding, more exciting or more important than that of teaching. We invite you to give teaching a try as soon as you can, as a tutor of younger children when you are still in school, if possible. You will see for yourself what a unique experience it is to give others the tools they need to master their future. We invite you to become the key to the nation's future — to its prosperity, to opportunity for all, to the maintenance of our democracy. You will have the whole nation behind you. It cannot be otherwise. There is too much at stake.

Comments

Comments

Statement of Support with Reservations
by Mary Hatwood Futrell

The Task Force on Teaching has identified several fundamental educational issues. The report reflects a full range of the competing interests and ideas of its members; I endorse many of those ideas wholeheartedly. I am particulary pleased that the report calls for additional funding for education, increased teacher salaries and status, enhanced teacher preparation standards, strategies to attract minority teachers to the profession, and teacher involvement in educational decision making.

At the same time, I have deep reservations about some of the report's conclusions and recommendations because they are inconsistent with what my years of experience in the classroom and as an NEA leader tell me will help students learn.

First, as a teacher, I am troubled that the report gives the impression that teachers are not doing their job. Capable teachers who exceed expectations described in the report already exist.

Second, while I have no fixed position about the proposed national standards board, I do strongly favor strengthening currently existing state standards boards and supporting creation of state standards boards in states where they do no now exist. Additionally, I would certainly want to see a distinct link between those state boards and the National Board.

Third, I am concerned about the potential for abuse in the Lead Teacher concept presented in the report. It suggests that some teachers are more equal than others. And it is not adequately differentiated from the flawed and failed merit pay and job ladder plans.

Fourth, I am committed to public education. I am committed to educational quality and equality for all. Some of the so-called market approaches outlined in this report such as vouchers and privately contracted teachers, could lead to quality for some, with a lesser quality for others . . . to full opportunity for some, but less opportunity for others. I believe the "market" for the public schools is every single American child — not just some special or select few. Every child deserves the opportunity to learn to his or her potential.

Fifth, the report concludes that there is no satisfactory method for measuring student performance and linking it to teachers' compensation. I agree. Therefore, I find inexplicable the report's emphasis upon such productivity measures. Further, effective teaching and student performance are very much related to class size, resources, and similar factors beyond teachers' control.

Sixth, I believe the report presumptions in advocating a singular model of teacher preparation — a graduate-level program — at a time when those who teach teachers are debating numerous ways to improve professional training. Further, no mention is made of the need for increased funding to teacher training programs.

Finally, the report fails to recognize current efforts. In fact, improvement efforts across the country are already meeting with some success. There is much we can do and must do today.

Statement of Support
by Albert Shanker

Now that the Task Force report is completed, I'm sure every member of the Task Force is going through an experience similar to my own. I am enthusiastic about the goals and vision of the report, though I would preferred to have had more of my ideas and differences withstand the Task Force process.

But, if one were to insist strictly on one's individual views, there really would be no Task Force report. The writing of a report by a task force is like negotiating a contract. When teachers criticize part of a contract I have helped negotiate, I tell them that I could have written a better one myself. But that's not what negotiations or task force reports are about. There are diverse groups, needs and interests represented at the table — just as there should be.

This report deserves full support. It promises to turn teaching into a full profession, make major structural changes in schools and take giant steps in the improvement of learning. Along with other memers of the Task Force who have refrained from expressing any differences in order to realize the greater goal, I give overall endorsement to the report.

Acknowledgements

Acknowledgements

We appreciate the leadership of David A. Hamburg in defining this new agenda, and especially value his counsel during our discussions, his confidence in our work throughout the past 12 months, and his commitment to act on the recommendations contained in this report.

The rapid progress made toward a consensus is largely due to the expert knowledge and courageous vision of the Carnegie Forum staff. Marc S. Tucker, Executive Director, and David R. Mandel, Associate Director, drafted the report through all its stages. More important, they were not afraid to challenge the Task Force with their own bold conceptions, while staying in touch with stake-holders in the outcome so the vision is both audacious and practical.

E. Alden Dunham, chair of the Corporation's Program on Education: Science, Technology, and the Economy, also made many contributions to our work. His perception of the importance of our endeavor and support as head of the foundation's major education grant program have proved invaluable.

We are indebted to all those who took the time, frequently at their own expense, to advise us in the course of this work. Without their cooperation, the Task Force could not have completed its charge, although we, of course, are responsible for any omissions or shortcomings in this report.

Many organizations and their leaders provided opportunities for Task Force members and Forum staff to present the evolving analysis and proposals, and provided constructive reactions that heavily influenced the shape of the final report. Among them are the American Association for Higher Education, the American Federation of Teachers, the Forum of Education Leaders, the National Association of Secondary School Principals, the National Association of State Boards of Education, the National Council of La Raza, the National Education Association, the National Elementary School Principals Association, the National School Boards Association and the National Urban League.

This Task Force has not been alone in producing major reports on teaching over the past year. Both the quality of our own work and the prospects for success for everyone have been greatly enhanced by a strong spirit of cooperation among the many organizations that have been engaged in the effort. We are particularly grateful to the National Governors' Association, the Education Commission of the States, the California Commission on the Teaching Profession, the Committee for Economic Development, the American Association of Colleges of Teacher Education, and the Holmes Group for their willingness to share data and views with us as we all worked toward a common goal.

The authors of the commissioned papers, among them some of the nation's most able scholars, set aside other obligations to take on the work we asked of them, and distinguished themselves with the work they produced on a grueling schedule.

We were greatly assisted by the attendees of two workshops convened by the Task

Force, one on education finance and another on school administration. Their names can be found in the appendix.

Kathy Devaney provided essential help in thinking about a professional environment for teaching. Richard Mills, Joe Nathan, and Joan Wills helped with implementation strategy. Marsha Levine researched examples of people already at work doing the things we advocate. The staff at the U.S. Department of Education's Center for Education Statistics regularly responded to our requests for data, informing our deliberations from the start. Many others, too numerous to list, have contributed in important ways to the ideas found in these pages, not least among these being teachers, both current and former, who took a special interest in the success of this endeavor.

Finally, we want to acknowledge the importance to our endeavor of the efforts of those without whom this report could not have been produced: Betsy Brown, Staff Associate of the Forum, who performed essential research tasks and orchestrated the endless details that made the Task Force meetings go smoothly; Cathy Combs, the Forum's Administrative Assistant, who supervised administrative operations; James Harvey and Bill Howard, who provided editorial assistance; and Lynn Hubsch, who designed the graphics and layout.

Appendices

Appendices

APPENDIX A:
CARNEGIE FORUM ADVISORY COUNCIL

David A. Hamburg, Chairman
President
Carnegie Corporation of New York
New York, New York

William O. Baker
Retired Chairman of the Board
AT&T Bell Telephone Laboratories
Murray Hill, New Jersey

Lewis M. Branscomb
Chief Scientist & Vice President
IBM Corporation
Armonk, New York

Henry G. Cisneros
Mayor
City of San Antonio
San Antonio, Texas

John W. Gardner
Writer and Consultant
Washington, D.C.

Fred M. Hechinger
President
The New York Times Company Foundation
New York, New York

James B. Hunt
Attorney
Poyner & Spruill
Raleigh, North Carolina

Donald Kennedy
President
Stanford University
Stanford, California

Margaret L.A. MacVicar
Vice President
Carnegie Institution of Washington
Washington, D.C.
Professor of Physical Science
Cecil and Ida Green Professor of Education
Dean for Undergraduate Education
Massachusetts Institute of Technology
Cambridge, Massachusetts

Shirley M. Malcom
Program Head
Office of Opportunities in Science
American Association for the
Advancement of Science
Washington, D.C.

Ray Marshall
Bernard Rapoport Centennial Chair in
Economics & Public Affairs
L.B.J. School of Public Affairs
University of Texas
Austin, Texas

Shirley M. McBay
Dean for Student Affairs
Massachusetts Institute of Technology
Cambridge, Massachusetts

Michael O'Keefe
President
Consortium for the Advancement of Private
Higher Education
Washington, D.C.

Mary Louise Petersen
President Emeritus
Iowa State Board of Regents
Des Moines, Iowa

Ruth E. Randall
Commissioner of Education
State of Minnesota
Saint Paul, Minnesota

Peter Smith
Lieutenant Governor of Vermont
Montpelier, Vermont

John C. Taylor, 3rd
Executive Vice President
AEA Investors
New York, New York

Robert M. White
President
National Academy of Engineering
Washington, D.C.

William S. Woodside
Chief Executive Officer and Chairman of the
Board
American Can Company
Greenwich, Connecticut

APPENDIX B:
PAPERS COMMISSIONED FOR THE
CARNEGIE FORUM'S TASK FORCE ON TEACHING AS A PROFESSION

Black Participation in the Teacher Pool
Joan C. Baratz, Director, Division of Education Policy Research and Services, Educational Testing Service

The Gains From Education Reform
Stephen M. Barro, President, SMB Economic Research

Current Approaches to Teacher Assessment
Tom Bird, Project Director, Far West Laboratory

School Resource Allocations: Potential for Change
Frederick Dembowski, Associate Professor, Frances Kemmerer, Research Associate, and Alan P. Wagner, Research Associate, Center for Educational Research and Policy Studies, School of Education, State University of New York at Albany

Teacher Choice: Does it Have a Future?
Denis P. Doyle, Director, Education Policy Studies, American Enterprise Institute for Public Policy Research

Students as Teachers: A Tool for Improving School Climate and Productivity
Diane Hedin, Associate Professor and Assistant Director, Center for Youth Development and Research, University of Minnesota

Teacher Mobility and Pension Portability
Bernard Jump Jr., Professor and Chairman, Department of Public Administration, and Associate Dean, Maxwell School, Syracuse University

Financing Education Reform
James A. Kelly, President, Center for Creative Studies

Increasing the Number and Quality of Minority Science and Mathematics Teachers
Shirley M. McBay, Dean for Student Affairs, Massachusetts Institute of Technology

A National Board for Teaching? In Search of a Bold Standard
Lee S. Shulman, Professor of Education, and Gary Sykes, Research Associate, Stanford University

The Knowledge Base for Teaching
Lee S. Shulman, Professor of Education, Stanford University

Professional Examinations: A Cross Occupational Analysis
Gary Sykes, Research Associate, Stanford University

APPENDIX C:
WORKSHOP PARTICIPANTS

Education Finance Workshop
December 18–19, 1985

Charles Benson
School of Education
University of California
Berkeley, California

Lewis M. Branscomb
Vice President and Chief Scientist
IBM Corporation
Armonk, New York

Anthony P. Carnevale
Vice President,
Governmental Affairs
American Society for Training and
  Development
Alexandria, Virginia

E. Alden Dunham
Program Chair
Carnegie Corporation of New York
New York, New York

Margaret Goertz
Senior Research Scientist
Education Policy Research and Services
Educational Testing Service
Princeton, New Jersey

Steven D. Gold
Program Director, Fiscal Affairs
National Conference of State Legislators
Denver, Colorado

James A. Kelly
President
Center for Creative Studies
Detroit, Michigan

Helen Ladd
Department of City and Regional Planning
Harvard University
Cambridge, Massachusetts

Will Myers
Manager, School Finance
National Education Association
Washington, D.C.

Allan Odden
Department of Education Policy
University of Southern California
Los Angeles, California

William Spring
Vice President
District Community Affairs
Federal Reserve Bank of Boston
Boston, Massachusetts

Robert Reischauer
Vice President
The Urban Institute
Washington, D.C.

School Administration Workshop
February 18, 1986

Eve Bither
Superintendent
Freeport Public Schools
Freeport, Maine

Raymon Cortines
Superintendent
San Jose Unified School District
San Jose, California

Michael Hickey
Superintendent
Howard County Public School System
Ellicott City, Maryland

Harry Jaroslaw
Superintendent
Morris Board of Education
Morristown, New Jersey

Floretta McKenzie
Superintendent
District of Columbia Public Schools
Washington, D.C.

Douglas Magann
Superintendent
Alachua County Schools
Gainsville, Florida

Shirley Malcom
Program Head
Office of Opportunities in Science
American Association for the Advancement of
Science
Washington, D.C.

Bruce Richardson
Superintendent
Orleans Southwest School District
Hardwick, Vermont

Jay Robinson
Superintendent
Charlotte-Mecklenberg Schools
Charlotte, North Carolina

Robert Schwartz
Assistant to the Superintendent
Boston Public Schools
Boston, Massachusetts

Anthony Trujillo
Superintendent
Sweetwater Union High School District
Chula Vista, California

Saul Yanofsky
Assistant to the Superintendent
White Plains Public Schools
White Plains, New York

APPENDIX D:
BIOGRAPHICAL SKETCHES

The Task Force

Lewis M. Branscomb, Chairman

Lewis M. Branscomb is Vice President and Chief Scientist of International Business Machines Corporation and a member of its Corporate Management Board. A research physicist, Dr. Branscomb was appointed Director of the National Bureau of Standards in 1969 by President Nixon, having worked at the Bureau since 1951. After being named Chairman of the National Science Board by President Carter in 1980, Dr. Branscomb launched the Board's Commission on Precollege Education in Mathematics, Science and Technology. Dr. Branscomb was a founding trustee of the North Carolina School for Mathematics and Science, and chairs the Education Relations Board of IBM. Dr. Branscomb serves as a member of the Carnegie Forum's Advisory Council.

Alan K. Campbell

Alan K. Campbell is Executive Vice-President and Vice-Chairman of ARA Services, Incorporated. As Chairman of the Civil Service Commission and first Director of the Office of Personnel Management during the Carter Administration, Dr. Campbell oversaw the reform of the Federal civil service system. A political economist, he has held numerous professorships including Dean of the Maxwell School of Citizenship and Public Affairs at Syracuse University, and of the LBJ School of Public Affairs at the University of Texas. Mr. Campbell was a member of the Committee for Economic Development's Research Advisory Committee and chaired their Task Force on the Teaching Profession. He was a member of the Business Advisory Commission of the Education Commission of the States, and Chairman of the Board of Public/Private Ventures, an organization devoted to the employment and training of at-risk youths.

Mary Hatwood Futrell

Mary Hatwood Futrell has been President of the National Education Association since 1983. A high school business education teacher from Alexandria, Virginia, she has worked with the National Assessment of Educational Progress and is an active member of the Carnegie Foundation's National Panel on the Study of the American High School. In 1981, Mrs. Futrell was appointed by the Reagan Administration to the U.S. National Commission for the United Nations Education, Scientific, and Cultural Organization (UNESCO) and, in 1984, was elected to the executive committee of the World Confederation of Organizations of the Teaching Profession. Mrs. Futrell serves on the Educational Advisory Council for Metropoitan Life Insurance Company and on the Board of Trustees of the Joint Council on Economic Education.

John W. Gardner

John W. Gardner served as President Johnson's Secretary of Health, Education and Welfare from 1965 to 1968. At the time of his appointment to the Cabinet, Mr. Gardner had served as President of the Carnegie Corporation of New York and the Carnegie Foundation for the Advancement of Teaching for 10 years. Mr. Gardner was Chairman of President Kennedy's Commission on International Education and Cultural Affairs, and Chairman of President Johnson's Task Force on Education and of the 1965 White House Conference on Education. In 1970, he founded Common Cause and in 1978 he chaired the Organizing Committee that led to the founding of Independent Sector. Recently Mr. Gardner served on President Reagan's Task Force on Private Sector Initiatives. Mr. Gardner is now engaged in a five-year program of leadership studies under the sponsorship of Independent Sector, and serves as a member of the Carnegie Forum's Advisory Council. A psychologist, Mr. Gardner taught psychology at the University of California, Connecticut College for Women, and Mount Holyoke College.

Fred M. Hechinger

Fred M. Hechinger has been the President of the New York Times Company Foundation since 1977. The major areas in which the Foundation reviews applications for grants are education, journalism, cultural affairs, community services and environmental concerns. Mr. Hechinger serves as a board member for Carnegie Corporation of New York and the Academy for Educational Development and sits on the Carnegie Forum's Advisory Council. From 1950 to 1956, he was Associate Publisher and Executive Editor of The Bridgeport Sunday Herald, while also serving as Education Editor for Parents' Magazine. From 1959 to 1969, he was Education Editor of The New York Times. Mr. Hechinger became a member of the Editorial Board of The Times in 1969 and was Assistant Editor of the Editorial Page during 1976.

Bill Honig

Bill Honig has been Superintendent of Public Instruction for the State of California since his election in 1982. After pursuing a successful law career, Mr. Honig joined the Teacher Corps in 1971 and until 1976 worked as an elementary school teacher in Hunter's Point, an economically depressed area in the San Francisco Unified School District. From teaching, he moved on to become the Director of the San Francisco Foundation's staff development project where he helped design and conduct training programs for teachers and principals in the areas of curriculum and administration. Most recently, Mr. Honig served from 1979 to 1982 as Superintendent of the Reed Union Elementary School District in Marin County. As State Superintendent, he serves as the Executive Officer and Secretary of the California State Board of Education and as the Director of the State Department of Education.

James Baxter Hunt, Jr.

James Baxter Hunt, Jr., served as North Carolina's first two-term Governor, holding office from 1977 to 1985. His administration was marked by special attention to education, jobs, economic growth, and prison reform. Under his leadership, the North Carolina School of Science and Mathematics, the Microelectronics Center of North Carolina, and the North Carolina Business Committee for Education were all established. Governor Hunt has chaired the National Governors' Association Task Force on Technological Innovation, the Education Commission of the States and the Task Force on Education for Economic Growth that produced *Action for Excellence*, one of the major education reform reports of 1983. Before receiving his J.D. in 1964, Governor Hunt studied agricultural education and economics and served as a student teacher. From 1964 to 1966, he served as a Ford Foundation Economic Adviser to Nepal. Governor Hunt, now an attorney in private practice with the firm of Poyner and Spruill, is also a member of the Carnegie Forum's Advisory Council.

Vera Katz

Vera Katz is serving her seventh term in the Oregon House of Representatives and was elected Speaker of the House in January 1985. She is the first woman speaker in Oregon's legislative history and the only woman in the country currently holding that position. Speaker Katz served as Chair of the Fiscal Affairs and Oversight Committee for the National Conference of State Legislatures, and is currently Vice-Chair of the National Conference of State Legislatures' Assembly of the Legislatures. She developed Oregon's High Technology-Education Consortium, a public-private partnership of leaders in postsecondary education and high technology industries that established the state's educational Centers of Excellence. Speaker Katz is Director of Development at Portland Community College.

Thomas H. Kean

Thomas H. Kean recently began his second term as Governor of New Jersey, having been first elected in 1981. Since taking office, he has begun a number of new initiatives to create jobs, including cutting business taxes, improving job training, establishing urban enterprise zones, and increasing economic development investments. A former high school history teacher, Governor Kean has launched a program to upgrade the quality of New Jersey's schools by establishing minimum salaries for teachers, strengthening college teacher preparation programs, providing alternatives to traditional college-based certification, developing a teacher grant program to recognize excellent teachers and recruiting top high school graduates into the teaching field. He has served as Chairman of the Coalition of Northeastern Governors and is currently the Chairman of the Human Resources Committee of the National Governors' Association and of its Task Force on Teaching that is preparing "The 1991 Report." This year the Governor has also chaired the Education Commission of the States where he initiated the ECS' Teacher Renaissance Project. Governor Kean served in the New Jersey General Assembly from 1968 to 1977, and was Speaker of the Assembly from 1972 to 1974.

Judith E. Lanier

Judith E. Lanier is dean of the College of Education at Michigan State University. Founding co-Director of the Institute for Research on Teaching (IRT), she serves today as Associate Director of IRT concerned with the relationship between research and practice. Dr. Lanier is a member of the Holmes Group Consortium and chairs the group's steering committee. She also serves as the first Vice-President of the American Educational Research Association's recently formed Division on Teaching and Teacher Education. Dr. Lanier has taught in elementary, junior high and high school. Her scholarly activity focuses on the nexus between professional study in schools of education and professional practice in the elementary and secondary sector.

Arturo Madrid

Arturo Madrid is the first President of the Tomas Rivera Center, an institute for policy studies with a special focus on Hispanic issues that is affiliated with the Claremont Graduate School. Dr. Madrid is also President of the National Chicano Council on Higher Education. A Spanish and Portuguese professor, Dr. Madrid has held faculty appointments at Dartmouth College, the University of California, San Diego, and the University of Minnesota, where he served as Associate Dean and Executive Officer of the College of Liberal Arts. From 1975 to 1980 he directed the Ford Foundation's Graduate Fellowships Program for Mexican Americans, Native Americans and Puerto Ricans and during 1980 and 1981, served as Director of the U.S. Department of Education's Fund for the Improvement of Postsecondary Education in the Carter Administration. He is currently a trustee of the College Board.

Shirley M. Malcom

Shirley M. Malcom is Program Head of the Office of Opportunities in Science at the American Association for the Advancement of Science. Since 1980, Dr. Malcom has served as a member of the Executive Board of the Commission on Professionals in Science and Technology. From 1984 to 1986, Dr. Malcom served as the Chairperson of the National Science Foundation Committee on Equal Opportunities in Science and Technology and serves as a member of the Carnegie Forum's Advisory Council. From 1977 to 1979, Dr. Malcom was Program Manager of the Minority Institutions Science Improvement Program at the National Science Foundation. Dr. Malcom has been an Assistant Professor of Biology at the University of North Carolina and also taught high school science. Continuing a family tradition, Dr. Malcom joined her mother, sister, aunts and cousins as a member of the teaching profession.

Ruth E. Randall

Ruth E. Randall was appointed Minnesota's Commissioner of Education by Governor Perpich in 1983. Beginning in 1967 as an elementary school principal in Omaha, Nebraska, Commissioner Randall has held a variety of school administrative positions. Between 1978 and 1983, Commissioner Randall served as Assistant Superintendent of Personnel, Deputy Superintendent and finally Superintendent of Schools in Rosemount, Minnesota. Commissioner Randall has taught at all educational levels from elementary school through graduate school. Commissioner Randall was a founding member of Women Executives in State Government and serves as a member of the Carnegie Forum's Advisory Council.

Albert Shanker

Albert Shanker has been President of the American Federation of Teachers, AFL-CIO, since 1974 and, from 1964 until he stepped down earlier this year, of its New York City local, the United Federation of Teachers. Since 1981, he has also been President of the International Federation of Free Teachers' Unions (IFFTU), an organization of teacher unions in the democratic countries. Mr. Shanker is a Vice President of the AFL-CIO and sits on its Executive Council. He is President of the AFL-CIO Department of Professional Employees and serves as co-chair of the Municipal Labor Committee in New York City. Mr. Shanker's first exposure to the classroom was as a junior high school math teacher in the New York City schools.

THE STAFF

Marc S. Tucker

Marc S. Tucker is Executive Director of the Carnegie Forum on Education and the Economy. Mr. Tucker's career in education includes work on educational telecommunications, mathematics and science curriculum development and technical assistance to schools serving students from low-income families. He was at the National Institute of Education from 1972 through 1982, including four years as Associate Director for Educational Policy and Organization. Before joining Carnegie Corporation as a staff member, Mr. Tucker served as Director of the Project on Information Technology and Education.

David R. Mandel

David R. Mandel is Associate Director of the Carnegie Forum. He began working on education policy issues at the U.S. Office of Economic Opportunity. At the National Institute of Education from 1973 to 1982 his work included establishing research programs on school finance equalization, family choice mechanisms, human capital and postsecondary finance and governance. During his last four years at the Institute, he was the Assistant Director responsible for the Education Finance Program. Just prior to joining Carnegie Corporation, Mr. Mandel served as a Senior Policy Analyst in the Office of the Under Secretary of Education.

Catherine J. Combs

Catherine J. Combs is the Carnegie Forum's Administrative Assistant. She came to Carnegie Corporation from the National Organization for Women where she was secretary to the Vice President. Earlier in her career she worked for a nationally known architectural firm and George Washington University.

Betsy S. Brown

Betsy S. Brown is a Staff Associate with the Carnegie Forum. Before joining the staff of Carnegie Corporation, she was a Legislative Aide with the U.S. Senate Special Committee on Aging. Prior to her service in the Senate, Ms. Brown was Legislative Assistant to Gareth Wardell, a Member of Parliament, Great Britain.

Ordering Information / Publications Order Form

Publication	Price		Qty	Cost
THE REPORT OF THE TASK FORCE	1 - 10	$9.95 ea. ppd	_____	_____
1. *A Nation Prepared:*	11 - 25	$8.95 ea. ppd	_____	_____
Teachers for the 21st Century	26 +	$6.95 ea. ppd	_____	_____

Commissioned Papers $3.00 each postpaid

2. *Black Participation in the Teacher Pool,* Baratz _____ _____

3. *Teacher Choice: Does it Have a Future?* Doyle _____ _____

4. *Students as Teachers: A Tool for Improving School Climate and Productivity,* Hedin _____ _____

5. *Teacher Mobility and Pension Portability,* Jump _____ _____

6. *Financing Education Reform,* Kelly _____ _____

7. *Increasing the Number and Quality of Minority Science and Mathematics Teachers,* McBay _____ _____

8. *A National Board for Teaching? In Search of a Bold Standard,* Shulman and Sykes _____ _____

Total _____

The follwing MUST be completed to fill order:

NAME _____

TITLE _____

INSTITUTION _____

ADDRESS _____

_____

CITY _____

STATE _____ ZIP _____

TELEPHONE (_____)_____

Make purchase order or check payable to 'Carnegie Forum on Education and the Economy' and mail to:

Carnegie Forum
  on Education and the Economy
P.O. Box 157
Hyattsville, MD 20781